前 言

学习汉语的外国学生，当他们初步掌握了汉语的语音、词汇、语法和文字时，很想进一步提高自己的汉语水平。怎样提高呢?一件重要的事就是需要掌握一些汉语语言中最有特色的东西——例如典故、成语、谚语、歇后语。这些东西既和汉语汉字有密切关系，又和汉族的文化背景有密切关系。掌握了它们，不但能够丰富外国人汉语的表达能力，而且也能够增强他们汉语表达的民族特色。简而言之，他们所掌握的汉语就更像汉语了。这就为成为一个“中国通”迈出了重要的一步。

为以上目的，我们给这样的外国学生编了一套“博古通今学汉语丛书”，包括“典故 100”、“成语 100”、“谚语 100”和“歇后语 100”。

本套书精选汉语中最有价值的、常用的、表现力强的成语、谚语、歇后语、典故各 100 则。每则均附英文释义，每则配一幅精美插图，另有一些难解词语中英文注释。

Preface

What is the next step for a foreign student of the Chinese language after mastering the phonetics, grammar, and a fair amout of vocabulary? It is highly desirable to grasp something typical Chinese — like idioms, set phrases, proverbs or even the two-part allegorical sayings peculiar to Chinese. These idioms are so closely related to Chinese culture that once one has mastered them, one will not only be able to speak idiomatic Chinese and sound more like a native speaker does, but also penetrate deeper into Chinese culture, and gradually become a "China Hand".

For this purpose, we have composed this *Gems of the Chinese Language Through the Ages* series, which comprises the following four books:

The Stories Behind 100 Chinese Idioms
100 Pearls of Chinese Wisdom
100 Common Chinese Idioms and Set Phrases
100 Chinese Two-Part Allegorical Sayings

These idioms and proverbs have been chosen for their frequency of use, practical value and expressiveness. Each one is accompanied by an English translation and an appropriate illustration. Some obscure expressions are classified with the help of annotations in both Chinese and English.

目　　录
Contents

前言……………………………………………… *1*

Preface……………………………………………… *2*

1. 按图索骥……………………………………………… 1
   Looking for a Steed with the Aid of Its Picture
2. 百发百中……………………………………………… 3
   A Hundred Shots, a Hundred Bull's-Eyes
3. 班门弄斧……………………………………………… 5
   Showing Off One's Proficiency with the Axe Before Lu Ban the Master Carpenter
4. 杯弓蛇影……………………………………………… 7
   Mistaking the Reflection of a Bow for a Snake
5. 闭门造车……………………………………………… 9
   Building a Cart Behind Closed Doors
6. 病入膏肓……………………………………………… 11
   The Disease Has Attacked the Vitals
7. 草木皆兵……………………………………………… 13
   Every Bush and Tree Looks like an Enemy
8. 吹毛求疵……………………………………………… 15
   Blow Apart the Hairs upon a Fur to Discover Any Defect
9. 打草惊蛇……………………………………………… 17
   Beating the Grass and Flushing Out the Snake

10. 调虎离山……………………………………………… 19
Luring the Tiger Out of the Mountains
11. 东施效颦……………………………………………… 21
Aping the Beauty's Frown
12. 对牛弹琴……………………………………………… 23
Playing the Lute to a Cow
13. 负荆请罪……………………………………………… 25
Bringing the Birch and Asking for a Flogging
14. 功亏一篑……………………………………………… 27
Ruining an Enterprise for the Lack of One Basketful
15. 故步自封……………………………………………… 29
Content with Staying Where One Is
16. 含沙射影……………………………………………… 31
Spitting Sand on a Shadow-Attacking by Insinuation
17. 狐假虎威……………………………………………… 33
Basking in Reflected Glory
18. 囫囵吞枣……………………………………………… 35
Gulping Down a Whole Date
19. 画饼充饥……………………………………………… 37
Allaying Hunger with Pictures of Cakes
20. 画龙点睛……………………………………………… 39
Putting the Finishing Touch to the Picture of a Dragon
21. 画蛇添足……………………………………………… 41
Drawing a Snake and Adding Feet
22. 惊弓之鸟……………………………………………… 43
Birds Startled by the Mere Twang of a Bowstring
23. 精卫填海……………………………………………… 45

Jingwei Fills Up the Sea
24. 井底之蛙………………………………………………… 47
A Frog in a Well
25. 刻舟求剑………………………………………………… 49
Notching the Boat to Find the Sword
26. 空中楼阁………………………………………………… 51
A Castle in the Air
27. 滥竽充数………………………………………………… 53
Passing Oneself Off as a Member of the Orchestra
28. 狼狈为奸………………………………………………… 55
A Wolf Working Hand in Glove with a Jackal
29. 老马识途………………………………………………… 57
An Old Horse Knows the Way
30. 梁上君子………………………………………………… 59
A Gentleman on the Beam
31. 临渴掘井………………………………………………… 61
Not Digging a Well Until One Is Thirsty
32. 满城风雨………………………………………………… 63
A Storm Enveloping the City
33. 盲人摸象………………………………………………… 65
Blind Men Touching an Elephant
34. 毛遂自荐………………………………………………… 67
Mao Sui Recommending Himself
35. 门庭若市………………………………………………… 69
A Courtyard as Crowded as a Marketplace
36. 名落孙山………………………………………………… 71
Failing to Pass an Examination

37. 南辕北辙………………………………………… 73
Going South by Driving the Chariot North
38. 怒发冲冠………………………………………… 75
So Angry That One's Hair Lifts Up One's Hat
39. 披荆斩棘………………………………………… 77
Breaking Open a Way Through Brambles and Thorns
40. 蚍蜉撼树………………………………………… 79
An Ant Trying to Shake a Big Tree
41. 破釜沉舟………………………………………… 81
Smashing the Cauldrons and Sinking the Boats
42. 破镜重圆………………………………………… 83
A Broken Mirror Made Whole Again
43. 骑虎难下………………………………………… 85
When One Rides a Tiger It Is Hard to Dismount
44. 杞人忧天………………………………………… 87
The Man of Qi Who Worried That the Sky Would Fall
45. 黔驴技穷………………………………………… 89
The Guizhou Donkey Has Exhausted Its Tricks
46. 日暮途穷………………………………………… 92
The Day Is Waning and the Road Is Ending
47. 如火如荼………………………………………… 94
Like a Raging Fire
48. 如鱼得水………………………………………… 97
To Feel Just like a Fish in Water
49. 入木三分………………………………………… 99
To Enter Three-Tenths of an Inch into the Timber
50. 塞翁失马……………………………………… 101

The Old Man of the Frontier Lost His Horse
51. 三顾茅庐………………………………………… 103
Paying Three Visits to the Cottage
52. 三人成虎………………………………………… 105
Repeat a Lie Enough Times and It Will Be Believed
53. 丧家之犬………………………………………… 107
A Homeless Dog
54. 杀鸡吓猴………………………………………… 109
Killing the Chicken to Frighten the Monkeys
55. 甚嚣尘上………………………………………… 111
Making a Great Clamor
56. 势如破竹………………………………………… 113
Like Splitting Bamboo
57. 世外桃源………………………………………… 115
A Haven of Peace and Happiness
58. 手不释卷………………………………………… 117
Always with a Book in Hand
59. 守株待兔………………………………………… 119
Sitting by a Stump, Waiting for a Careless Hare
60. 蜀犬吠日………………………………………… 121
A Sichuan Dog Barks at the Sun
61. 束之高阁………………………………………… 123
Putting It on a High Shelf
62. 水落石出………………………………………… 125
When the Water Ebbs, Stones Will Appear
63. 四面楚歌………………………………………… 127
Songs of Chu on All Sides

64. 谈虎色变…………………………………… 129
Turn Pale at the Mention of a Tiger
65. 昙花一现…………………………………… 131
A Flower That Vanishes as Soon as It Appears
66. 螳臂当车…………………………………… 133
A Mantis Trying to Halt a Chariot
67. 天花乱坠…………………………………… 135
As If It Were Raining Flowers
68. 天涯海角…………………………………… 137
The End of the Sky and the Corner of the Sea
69. 天衣无缝…………………………………… 139
Divine Garments Without Seams
70. 同舟共济…………………………………… 141
Crossing a River in the Same Boat
71. 偷天换日…………………………………… 143
Stealing the Sky and Changing the Sun
72. 图穷匕见…………………………………… 145
When the Map Is Unrolled the Dagger Is Revealed
73. 完璧归赵…………………………………… 147
Returning the Jade Intact to Zhao
74. 亡羊补牢…………………………………… 149
Mending the Fold After the Sheep Have Been Stolen
75. 望梅止渴…………………………………… 151
Looking at Plums to Quench the Thirst
76. 望洋兴叹…………………………………… 153
Gazing at the Ocean and Sighing
77. 为虎作伥…………………………………… 155

Helping the Tiger to Pounce upon Its Victims
78. 卧薪尝胆…………………………………………………… 157
Sleeping on Brushwood and Tasting Gall
79. 笑里藏刀…………………………………………………… 159
Hiding a Dagger Behind a Smile
80. 胸有成竹…………………………………………………… 161
Having a Ready-Formed Plan
81. 削足适履…………………………………………………… 163
Cutting One's Feet to Fit One's Shoes
82. 揠苗助长…………………………………………………… 165
Pulling Up Seedlings to Help Them Grow
83. 掩耳盗铃…………………………………………………… 167
Plugging One's Ears While Stealing a Bell
84. 偃旗息鼓…………………………………………………… 169
To Lower the Banners and Silence the Drums
85. 叶公好龙…………………………………………………… 171
Lord Ye Loves Dragons
86. 夜郎自大…………………………………………………… 173
The Conceited King of Yelang
87. 一鼓作气…………………………………………………… 175
Rousing the Spirits with the First Drum Roll
88. 一箭双雕…………………………………………………… 177
Killing Two Birds with One Stone
89. 一鸣惊人…………………………………………………… 179
Amazing the World with a Single Feat
90. 一丘之貉…………………………………………………… 181
Jackals of the Same Lair

91. 愚公移山…………………………………………… 183
The Foolish Old Man Who Removed the Mountains
92. 鱼目混珠………………………………………… 185
Passing Off Fish Eyes as Pearls
93. 余音绕梁………………………………………… 187
The Tune Lingers in the House
94. 与虎谋皮………………………………………… 189
Borrowing the Skin from a Tiger
95. 鹬蚌相争………………………………………… 191
A Snipe and a Clam Locked in Combat
96. 朝三暮四………………………………………… 193
Three in the Morning and Four in the Evening
97. 趾高气扬………………………………………… 195
Stepping High and Haughtily
98. 指鹿为马………………………………………… 197
Calling a Stag a Horse
99. 纸上谈兵………………………………………… 199
Discussing Strategems on Paper
100. 自相矛盾………………………………………… 201
Contradicting Oneself

按图索骥

àn tú suǒ jì

Looking for a Steed with the Aid of Its Picture

春秋时代(公元前770—公元前476),秦国有个识马的能手,大家叫他"伯乐"。他把识别马的知识和经验,写成了一本书,还在书上配合文字画出了各种好马的形态。而他的儿子一点也不懂得识马的知识,只凭着书上画的图像去寻找好马,找来找去,一匹好马也没有找到。

"按图索骥"这个成语用来比喻没有实践经验、只知道机械地按老规矩办事。

In the Spring and Autumn Period (770 - 476 BC), there was a man in the State of Qin called Bo Le, who was an expert at judging horses. Based on his experience and knowledge of horses, he wrote a book in which he introduced the shapes and characteristics of fine horses both in words and illustrations. His son, having no first-hand experience of horses, set out to look for fine horses according to the instruction in the book. But he found none.

This idiom is used metaphorically to indicate lacking practical experience and doing things mechanically by following set rules.

骥:好马。

A splendid steed.

百发百中

bǎi fā bǎi zhòng

A Hundred Shots, a Hundred Bull's-Eyes

春秋时代,楚国有个人叫养由基,射箭的技术非常高超。有人在柳树上选择了高低不同的三片叶子,分别注上"一"、"二"、"三"的记号。养由基站在百步以外的地方,拉开弓,搭上箭,果然第一箭射中"一"叶,第二箭射中"二"叶,第三箭射中"三"叶,丝毫不差。

"百发百中"这个成语,形容射箭技术高超,每次都能命中。以后常常用来比喻做事有充分的把握,总能达到预期的目的。

In the Spring and Autumn Period, there was an expert archer in the State of Chu called Yang Youji. To test his skill, someone chose three leaves at different heights on a willow tree, and challenged him to hit them in order. Yang Youji stood more than one hundred paces away, and hit the three leaves in order.

This idiom describes excellent marksmanship. Later it became used to indicate great precision and perfect assurance.

班门弄斧

Bān mén nòng fǔ

Showing Off One's Proficiency with the Axe Before Lu Ban the Master Carpenter

古代有一个建筑和雕刻技术非常高超的人，名叫鲁班，木匠行里尊称他为祖师。传说他曾用木头制作了一只五彩斑斓（bānlán）的凤凰，能够在空中飞翔（xiáng）三天不掉下来。在鲁班门前摆弄斧子，当然显得有些自不量力了。

“班门弄斧”这个成语，用来比喻在行家面前显示本领。

Lu Ban was supposed to be a consummate carpenter in ancient times. It is said that he once carved a wooden phoenix that was so lifelike that it actually flew in the sky for three days. Thus it was considered the height of folly to show off one's skill with an axe in front of Lu Ban.

This idiom excoriates those who show off their slight accomplishments in front of experts.

杯弓蛇影

bēi gōng shé yǐng

Mistaking the Reflection of a Bow for a Snake

晋朝（公元265—420）时，有一个叫乐广的人，请他的朋友到家里喝酒。朋友端起酒杯喝酒的时候，忽然看见杯子里面有条小蛇的影子，他当时勉强将酒喝下。而回家后总是想起这件令人恶心的事，以至于生了病。乐广知道后，就把朋友再次请来，还是坐在原来的地方喝酒。那位朋友这才弄明白了，原来杯中的蛇影，是墙上挂着的一张弓映照出来的。事情弄明白了，病也就好了。

这个成语比喻疑神疑鬼，自相惊扰。

In the Jin Dynasty (265 - 420), a man called Yue Guang once invited a friend to have a drink at his home. When the friend lifted his cup, he saw a small snake in the wine, yet he forced himself to drink. Back home, the friend recalled the incident, and felt so disgusted that he fell ill. Hearing about this, Yue Guang invited his friend again. He asked him to sit in the same place and drink. Then his friend saw that the image of the snake in the cup was actually the reflection of a bow hung on the wall. Realising this, the friend recovered quickly.

This idiom indicates a condition of being over-suspicious bringing trouble on oneself.

闭门造车

bì mén zào chē

Building a Cart Behind Closed Doors

古时候,有一个人想造一辆很精巧的车子。他不去学习别人制造车子的实际经验，却把自己关在家里冥(míng)思苦想。费了很多功夫,车子虽然造好了,但是推出去却不能使用。

这个成语比喻只凭主观想象办事，不顾客观实际,结果总是碰壁。

In ancient times, there was a man who wanted to make a fine chariot. But, instead of learning how to do it from experts, he shut himself up at home and worked at it. Despite the time and effort he spent on it, the chariot was useless.

This idiom is used metaphorically to mean being too subjective and disregarding the rest of the world.

病入膏肓

bìng rù gāo huāng

The Disease Has Attacked the Vitals

春秋时候，晋景公生了病。病中梦见自己的疾病变成两个小人在他旁边谈话。一个说："我害怕医生会伤害我们。"另一个说："不要怕，我们躲到肓的上面，膏的下面，医生能把我们怎样！"第二天，医生来给他诊断病情时说："你的病没法子治啦！病在肓的上面，膏的下面，药剂的效力无法到达了。"

这个成语比喻事情已经非常严重，到了不可挽救的程度。

In the Spring and Autumn Period, King Jing of the State of Jin fell ill. One night he dreamed that the disease turned into two small figures talking beside him. One said, "I'm afraid the doctor will hurt us." The other said, "Don't worry. We can hide above *huang* and below *gao*. Then the doctor will be able to do nothing to us." The next day, having examined the king, the doctor said, "Your disease is incurable, I am afraid, Your Majesty. It's above *huang* and below *gao*, where no medicine can reach."

This idiom indicates a hopeless condition.

膏：心尖脂肪。

Fat around the heart.

肓：心脏和膈膜之间。

The area between the heart and the diaphragm.

草木皆兵

cǎo mù jiē bīng

Every Bush and Tree Looks like an Enemy

公元383年，前秦国王苻坚带了80万大军攻打东晋。在淝水一带，被晋朝大将谢玄的前锋部队打得大败。苻坚登上寿阳城，看见晋军阵容严整，心里害怕起来。再远望八公山上长着许多草和树木，也以为是东晋的士兵，更加惊恐万分。后来苻坚终于全军覆没（fùmò），带着少数残余的队伍逃了回去。

这个成语用来形容人在极度惊恐时，疑神疑鬼的心理状态。

In AD 383, the king of Former Qin, Fu Jian, led a huge army to attack Eastern Jin. After losing the first round of fighting, Fu Jian looked down from a city wall, and was terrified when he saw the formidable battle array of the Eastern Jin army. And then looking at the mountains around, he mistook the grass and trees for enemy soldiers. As a result, when the nervous Fu Jian led his army into battle, it suffered a crushing defeat.

This idiom describes how one can defeat oneself by imagining difficulties.

皆：都是。

All.

吹毛求疵

chuī máo qiú cī

Blow Apart the Hairs upon a Fur to Discover Any Defect

古时候，有一个专门喜欢寻找小毛病的人。有一次他到商店里去买兽皮。为了检查这张兽皮是不是一张好皮，就吹开兽皮上面的毛，一处一处地寻找里面的小毛病。

后来人们用这个成语比喻故意挑剔(tī)毛病，寻找差错。

In ancient times there was a man who was a notorious nitpicker. Once he went to buy a fur cloak. To check the fur, he blew the hairs apart, looking for trivial defects.

This idiom came to be used to describe looking for tiny faults.

疵：毛病。

Fault, defect.

打草惊蛇

dǎ cǎo jīng shé

Beating the Grass and Flushing Out the Snake

古时候有一个县官，贪污受贿（huì），谋取私利。有一次，有人写了一个状子，控告他的秘书贪污受贿。这个县官一边看状子，一边直打寒颤（zhàn）。他在状子后面写了八个字："汝（rǔ）虽打草，吾已惊蛇。"（"你虽然打的是地上的草，但我就象伏在草里面的蛇，已经受到惊吓了。"）

这个成语比喻做机密的事行动不小心，使对方觉察后有所防备。

In ancient times there was a county magistrate who took bribes and practised graft. One day, somebody sent him a petition accusing his secretary of practising graft and taking bribes. The magistrate trembled when he read the petition. He wrote on it: "You have beaten the grass and frightened a snake."

This idiom refers to alerting the target of one's scheme by being incautious.

调虎离山

diào hǔ lí shān

Luring the Tiger Out of the Mountains

老虎是居住在深山里的凶猛野兽。如果用计策引诱老虎离开了深山，人们就比较容易制服它了。

“调虎离山”这个成语，常常用来比喻使用计策，引诱人离开有利的环境，以便于控制或消灭他们。

The tiger is a ferocious animal which lives in the mountains. Only by luring it away from the mountains, can one subdue it.

This idiom is used metaphorically to mean enticing an enemy away from his safe haven in order to put him at a disadvantage.

东施效颦

Dōngshī xiào pín

Aping the Beauty's Frown

春秋时代,越国有个美女叫做西施。西施有胸口痛的病,病发作的时候,捧着胸口,皱着眉头。村子里有一个丑女子，叫做东施，觉得这个姿态很美，于是也学西施的样子捧着胸口，皱着眉头走路。她自己以为很美，其实这样一来却更显得丑了,连行人看见了都躲得远远的。

后来人们用“东施效颦”这个成语比喻不恰当的模仿,带来相反的效果。

In the Spring and Autumn Period, there was a beauty in the State of Yue called Xishi. She often suffered from pains in her chest, and so she would often walk around doubled over and with her brows knitted. There was an ugly girl in the village called Dongshi who envied Xishi. Striving to emulate Xishi, she imitated her stoop, knitting her brows at the same time. She thought that this made her elegant, but, in fact, it only made her more ugly.

Later, this idiom came to be used to indicate improper imitation that produces the reverse effect.

颦:皱眉。

To knit one's brow.

对牛弹琴

duì niú tán qín

Playing the Lute to a Cow

古时候，有一个人琴弹得很好。一次，他对着牛弹了一段曲子，希望牛也来欣赏他的技巧。曲子虽然很好听，但是牛却丝毫不理会，只顾埋头吃草。这个人没法，只好摇摇头叹了口气。

“对牛弹琴”这个成语，比喻对不懂道理的人讲道理。也用来讥笑说话的人不看对象。

In ancient times there was a man who played the zither very well. Once, he played a tune in front of a cow, hoping that the cow would appreciate it. The tune was melodious, but the cow showed no reaction, and just kept on eating grass. The man sighed, and went away.

This idiom is used to indicate reasoning with stubborn people or talking to the wrong audience.

负荆请罪

fù jīng qǐngzuì

Bringing the Birch and Asking for a Flogging

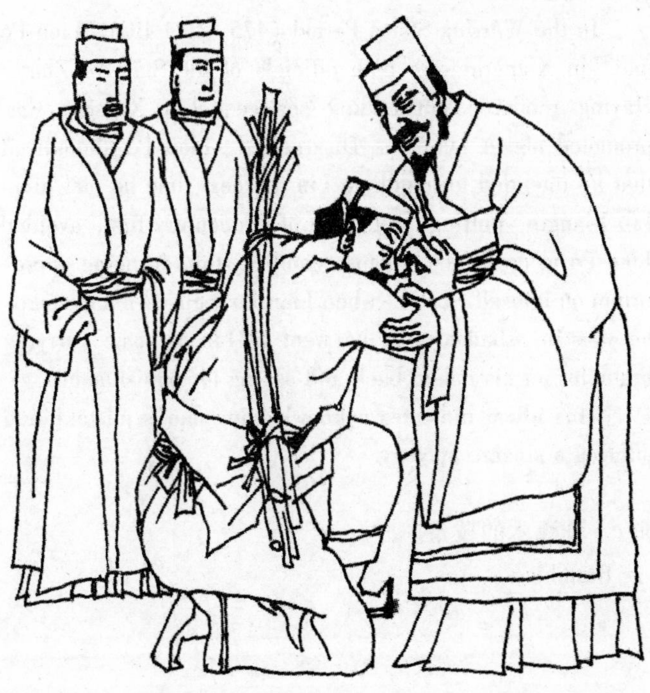

战国(公元前475—公元前221)时,廉(Lián)颇和蔺(Lìn)相如同在赵国作官。蔺相如立了大功,被封为上卿(qīng),官位比廉颇大。廉颇不服气,扬言要当面羞辱蔺相如。蔺相如为了国家的利益,处处避让,不与他相斗。后来廉颇认识到自己的错误,感到十分惭愧,便脱掉上衣,背上荆条,到蔺相如家里当面请罪。

"负荆请罪"这个成语用来表示向别人赔礼、认错。

In the Warring States Period (475 - 221 BC), Lian Po and Lin Xiangru were both officials of the State of Zhao. Having rendered outstanding service, Lin Xiangru was promoted above Lian Po. Disgruntled, Lian Po announced that he intended to humiliate Lin the next time he met him. Lin Xiangru, putting the benefit of the country first, avoided Lian Po in order not to cause conflict, thus bringing opprobrium on himself. Later, when Lian Po realised his mistake, he was so ashamed that he went to Lin's home carrying brambles on his naked back and asking for punishment.

This idiom indicates acknowledging one's mistake and offering a sincere apology.

荆:一种灌木的枝条。

Brambles.

功亏一篑

gōng kuī yī kuì

Ruining an Enterprise for the Lack of One Basketful

从前有一个人,打算修建一座土台。他辛辛苦苦地挖土、搬土,费了很多功夫,眼看土台快要修建成了。可是到了最后,只差一“篑”(盛土的筐子)土的时候,他不愿意干了。土台最终没有修建好。

“功亏一篑”这个成语被人们用来比喻事情即将完成,却不能坚持到底。含有惋惜的意思。

Once a man planned to build a terrace. He worked very hard and spent a lot of time digging and carrying earth. When the mound was almost completed and only one more basket of earth was needed, the man gave up. The terrace was never completed.

This idiom means to fail to succeed for lack of a final effort. It has a connotation of pity.

篑:盛土的筐子。

A basket for carrying earth.

故步自封

gù bù zì fēng

Content with Staying Where One Is

从前有一个人，想到很远的地方去。可是，他举起步来，总是在老路上转圈子。走啊，走啊，算起来已经应该走了很远的路了。可是一看，还是停留在原来的老地方。

“故步自封”这个成语比喻一个人老是停留在原地，安于现状，不求进取。

Once upon a time, a certain man wanted to go to a distant place. But he kept on walking in circles. After a long time, he thought he must have travelled a great distance. But when he looked around, he found that he was still at the starting point.

This idiom is used to describe those who are content with things as they are, and are not eager to make progress.

故：旧，从前。

Old, before.

封：限制在某一范围。

Limited within a range.

含沙射影

hán shā shè yǐng

Spitting Sand on a Shadow-Attacking by Insinuation

传说水里面有一种虫，名叫蜮(yù)。它头上有角，背上有甲，没有眼睛，长了三只脚，有翅膀能飞，嘴里有一个像弩(nǔ)一样的东西。如果听见人的脚步声，它就用嘴含着细沙朝人射来，人或者人的影子要是被射中(zhòng)了，就会生病。

“含沙射影”这个成语用来比喻在暗地里对人进行诽谤、中(zhòng)伤。

Legend has it that there was once a water monster called Yu. It had horns, a shell, wings and three legs, but no eyes. There was a catapult in its mouth. If Yu heard the steps of a man, it would shoot sand from its mouth at him. If even the man's shadow was hit, the man would fall ill.

This idiom indicates vilifying people by insinuation.

狐假虎威

hú jiǎ hǔ wēi

Basking in Reflected Glory

老虎在山林里捉到了一只狐狸,要吃掉它。狐狸连忙说:“你不能吃我,我是天帝派来统治百兽的。你要吃了我,就违抗了天帝的命令。你不信,就跟我到山林里去一趟,看百兽见了我是不是都很害怕。”老虎相信了狐狸的话,就跟在狐狸的后面走进山林。百兽见了果然都纷纷逃命。老虎以为百兽真的害怕狐狸而不知道是害怕自己,于是就把狐狸给放了。

“狐假虎威”这个成语用来比喻倚仗别人的势力去欺压人或吓唬人。

A tiger caught a fox in a forest, and was just about to eat it, when the fox said, “You mustn't eat me. I was sent by Heaven to rule the animals. By eating me, you will violate the command of Heaven. If you don't believe me, just follow me to see whether the animals are afraid of me.” The tiger agreed, and followed the fox as it walked around the forest. The animals all ran away on seeing them. The tiger thought they were afraid of the fox, so he let it go. He didn't realise that it was him that the beasts were really afraid of.

This idiom means relying on another's power to bully or frighten others.

假:借用。

To borrow.

囫囵吞枣

húlún tūn zǎo

Gulping Down a Whole Date

有一个医生向人介绍枣子的性能时说："枣子对人的脾脏(pízàng)有益，但是对牙齿有害。"旁边有一个人听了以后就说："我有一个好办法：吃枣子的时候不用牙齿嚼(jiáo)，一口吞下去，这样不就可以利用它的益处而避免它的害处了吗？"

以后人们就根据这个故事，把读书或理解事情不加分析、笼统地接受下去的行为叫做"囫囵吞枣"。

A physician once told a group of people: "Dates are good for the spleen, but harmful for the teeth." On hearing this, one man said, "I have a good idea: When eating dates, we should just swallow them whole without chewing them. Then we can both enjoy the advantage and avoid the disadvantage."

This story gave rise to the above idiom, which refers to lapping up information without digesting it, or reading without understanding or analysing.

囫囵：整个儿。

Entirely.

画饼充饥

huà bǐng chōng jī

Allaying Hunger with Pictures of Cakes

三国时代魏国的皇帝曹睿（ruì），准备选拔一个有才能的人到朝廷来做官。曹睿对他的大臣说："选择人才，不能光找有虚名的人。虚名好象是在地上画的一块饼，只能看，不能解决肚子饥饿的问题啊！"

后来人们就用"画饼充饥"这个成语比喻用空想安慰自己，不能解决实际问题。

In the Three Kingdoms Period (220-280), the king of the State of Wei, Cao Rui, wanted to select a very capable man to work for him. He said to his ministers: "When choosing a talented person, always beware of one with a false reputation. A false reputation is just like a picture of a cake; it can't relieve hunger."

Later, this idiom came to be used to mean comforting oneself with unrealistic thoughts, without solving practical problems.

画龙点睛

huà lóng diǎn jīng

Putting the Finishing Touch to the Picture of a Dragon

南北朝（公元420—589）时期，有个画家叫张僧繇（yóu）。有一次，他到一个寺庙去游玩，在墙壁上面画了四条龙，可是都没有画出眼睛。看画的人觉得很奇怪，问他为什么不画出眼睛。他说："眼睛是龙的关键，画上眼睛，龙就会飞走了。"大家不相信他说的话。张僧繇拿起笔来，刚给两条龙点上眼睛，立刻电闪雷鸣，两条龙飞向天空，墙上只剩下两条没有画眼睛的龙。

"画龙点睛"这个成语用来比喻讲话或写文章时，在关键地方加一两句重要的话，使内容更加生动有力。

In the Southern and Northern Dynasties Period (420-589), there was a painter called Zhang Zengyou. Once he visited a temple and painted on the wall four dragons, but gave none of them eyes. The onlookers felt that this was odd, and asked why he hadn't painted the eyes. He answered, "Eyes are crucial for dragons. With the eyes painted on, the dragons would fly away." Nobody believed this, so Zhang Zengyou took up his brush and added eyes to two of the dragons. No sooner had he finished than the two dragons flew into the sky amid a thunderstorm. The two without eyes stayed painted on the wall.

This idiom is used to describe how, when writing or speaking, one or two key sentences will enhance the contents.

画蛇添足

huà shé tiān zú

Drawing a Snake and Adding Feet

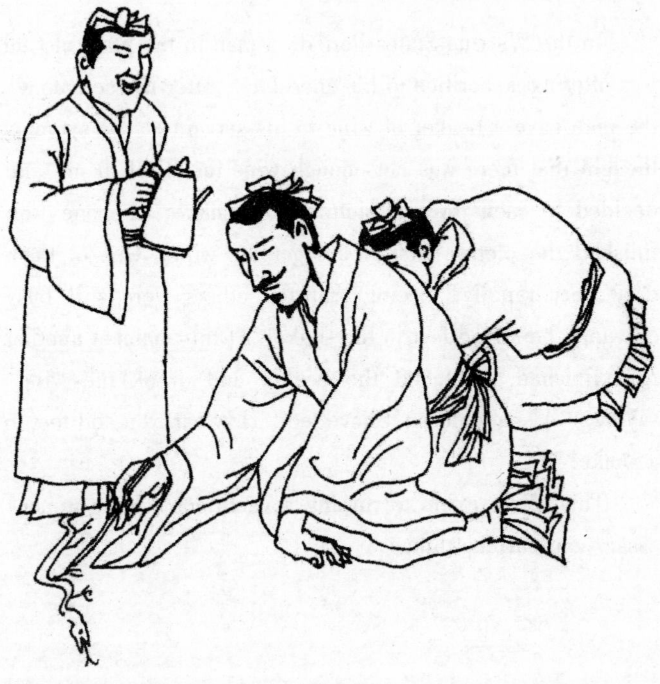

战国时代有个楚国人祭(jì)他的祖先。仪式结束后,他拿出一壶酒赏给手下的几个人。大家商量说:“我们都来画蛇,谁先画好谁就喝这壶酒。”其中有一个人先画好了。但他看到同伴还没有画完,就又给蛇添上了脚。这时,另一个人也画好了,夺过酒壶把酒喝了,并且说:“蛇本来是没有脚的,你怎么能给它添上脚呢?”

“画蛇添足”这个成语比喻做了多余而不恰当的事,反而把事情弄糟了。

In the Warring States Period, a man in the State of Chu was offering a sacrifice to his ancestors. After the ceremony, the man gave a beaker of wine to his servants. The servants thought that there was not enough wine for all of them, and decided to each draw a picture of a snake; the one who finished the picture first would get the wine. One of them drew very rapidly. Seeing that the others were still busy drawing, he added feet to the snake. At this moment another man finished, snatched the beaker and drank the wine, saying, “A snake doesn't have feet. How can you add feet to a snake?”

This idiom refers to ruining a venture by doing unnecessary and surplus things.

惊弓之鸟

jīng gōng zhī niǎo

Birds Startled by the Mere Twang of a Bowstring

战国时期魏国有个名叫更羸(léi)的人。一天，他对国王说："我只要拉开弓，空射一下，就能把天上的鸟射下来。"国王不相信。更羸便对准天上飞来的一只雁射去，果真那只雁听到拉弦的声音就掉了下来。国王感到很奇怪。更羸说："那是一只受过伤的雁。它一听到我拉开弓弦的声响，就惊慌得支持不住，自然要掉下来了。"

"惊弓之鸟"这个成语比喻受过惊恐之后，有一点动静就特别害怕。

In the Warring States Period, there was a man in the State of Wei called Geng Lei. One day he said to the king: "I can shoot down birds by simply plucking my bowstring." When the king expressed doubt, Geng Lei pointed his bow at a wild goose flying in the sky, twanged the bowstring, and the goose fell to the ground. Geng Lei said, "This goose has been hurt in the past. Hearing the twang of the bowstring, it assumed that it was doomed. So it simply gave up trying to live."

This idiom means that if one has been frightened in the past one's will may become paralysed in a similar situation.

精卫填海

jīngwèi tián hǎi

Jingwei Fills Up the Sea

传说在远古时代，炎帝有一个女儿，一天到东海去玩，不小心掉在海里淹死了。死后她变成了一只坚强、勇敢而美丽的小鸟，每天总是“精卫！精卫……”地叫，人们便叫她“精卫鸟”。她每天衔(xián)来西山上的木头或石头，投到东海里，决心要把东海填平。

“精卫填海”这个成语，比喻不怕艰难困苦，不达目的誓不罢休的坚强意志。

It is said that in remote antiquity King Yan had a daughter. One day she went to the East Sea to play, and was accidentally drowned. After her death she became a brave and beautiful bird, and was called the *jingwei* bird, in imitation of her cry. She was determined to fill up the sea. So every day she would pick up twigs and pebbles from the East Mountain and drop them into the sea.

This idiom describes an indomitable will to achieve one's goal regardless of all difficulties.

井底之蛙

jǐng dǐ zhī wā

A Frog in a Well

水井里居住着一只青蛙，从来没有到外面去游玩过。一天，东海来了一只鳖(biē)。青蛙非常得意地对它谈论起井底的“世界”是多么宽阔和美妙，并且邀(yāo)请鳖到井中来做客。鳖刚要进去，一只腿就被水井边的石头卡住了。于是，鳖把海洋如何宽广的情形讲给青蛙听。青蛙听了大吃一惊，感到非常惭愧。

“井底之蛙”这个成语用来讥笑人眼界狭小，见识短浅。

At the bottom of a well there lived a frog, which had never left the well in its life. One day he was visited by a turtle from the East Sea. The frog boasted to the turtle about the wideness and fineness of the well. But when the turtle told the frog about the sea, the frog felt humbled.

This idiom is used to satirize those who are shallow or narrow-minded.

刻舟求剑

kè zhōu qiú jiàn

Notching the Boat to Find the Sword

战国时期有个楚国的人，得到一把宝剑，非常珍爱。一天，他坐船过江，不小心把宝剑掉到江中去了。他急忙在剑掉下去的船舷（xián）边上刻了一个记号，说："我的剑是从这里掉下去的。"船靠岸后，他就从刻有记号的地方跳下水去找他的剑。船已经开走了，而剑并不能跟着船走，他怎么能找到宝剑呢？

"刻舟求剑"这个成语讽刺那些办事迂腐，不知道变通情况的人。

In the Warring States Period, a man in the State of Chu had a sword which he cherished very much. One day, when he was crossing a river in a boat, the sword suddenly fell into the water. The man then made a mark on the side of the boat at the spot where the sword had fallen overboard. When the boat reached the shore, he jumped from the spot he marked into the water to look for his sword.

This idiom satirizes those who stick to rigid rules instead of taking changed circumstances into account.

空中楼阁

kōngzhōng lóugé

A Castle in the Air

一个有钱人要建筑师给他盖一座三层高的楼房。建筑师照着他的吩咐，挖土动工。第一层刚盖好，准备盖第二层的时候，这个有钱人却对建筑师说："我只要你盖第三层，而不要第一层和第二层！"建筑师说："没有第一层和第二层，怎么能修建第三层呢！"说完摇摇头拿上他的工具就走了。

"空中楼阁"这个成语比喻脱离实际、近乎幻想的理论或计划等。

A rich man asked an architect to build a three-story house for him. When the first story was finished, the rich man said to the architect: "I want only the third story; not the first and second stories." The architect asked, "But without the first and second stories, how can I build the third story?" Shaking his head, he packed up his things, and left.

This idiom indicates an unrealistic or impractical plan or theory.

滥竽充数

làn yú chōng shù

Passing Oneself Off as a Member of the Orchestra

战国时代，齐宣王非常喜欢听吹竽，而且每次总要三百人同时吹。有一个南郭先生，本来不会吹竽，也混在中间凑数。后来，齐宣王死了，他的儿子齐湣（mǐn）王继位。湣王不喜欢听很多人同时吹竽，而要听一个人一个人地吹。南郭先生知道自己没办法再混下去，就偷偷地溜走了。

"滥竽充数"这个成语比喻没有本领而冒充有本领，或者拿次货冒充好货。

In the Warring States Period, King Xuan of the State of Qi loved to listen to the *yu*—an ancient wind instrument. He would order 300 musicians at a time to play the *yu* for him. Mr Nan Guo, who couldn't play the instrument, passed himself off as one of the musicians. When King Xuan died, his son King Min succeeded to the throne. King Min also loved *yu*, but he preferred solo performances. Mr Nan Guo thereupon slipped away from the orchestra.

This idiom is used to describe those who have no actual skills but pretend to be experts, or the passing off of inferior things as high-quality ones.

狼狈为奸

láng bèi wéi jiān

A Wolf Working Hand in Glove with a Jackal

狼和狈常常结伴出外伤害牲畜。有一次,狼和狈一起来到一个羊圈外面。羊圈很高,又很坚固,叼不走里面的羊。狼和狈就想了一个办法:因为狼的前脚长后脚短,狈的前脚短后脚长,狼骑在狈的颈上,狈用长长的后脚站起来,狼就用长长的前脚攀(pān)住羊圈,终于把羊叼走。

"狼狈为奸"这个成语比喻坏人互相勾结起来干坏事。

A wolf and a jackal often went hunting together. Once they came to a sheepfold the walls of which were firmly built and too high for them to get over. Then they had an idea: Since the wolf had long forelegs and short hindlegs while the jackal had short forelegs and long hindlegs, the wolf stood on the neck of the jackal, and the jackal stood up on its hindlegs. In this way the wolf climbed over the wall to where the sheep were.

This idiom is used to describe doing evil things in collusion with others.

老马识途

lǎo mǎ shí tú

An Old Horse Knows the Way

春秋时代,齐桓公出征攻打北方一个小国。去的时候是春天,遍地绿草茵茵。回来的时候是冬天,白雪茫茫,狂风怒吼,于是齐桓公的队伍迷失了方向。找不到回去的路,大家都很着急。这时,齐桓公的宰相管仲说:“可以利用老马的经验。”于是齐桓公派人挑选了几匹老马在前面引路,果然走出了迷谷,找到了回去的道路。

“老马识途”这个成语用来比喻有经验的人,熟悉情况,办事效果好。

In the Spring and Autumn Period, Duke Huan of Qi led an army to attack a small state in the north. They went in spring when green grass covered the ground. But when they came back it was winter. Everywhere was white with snow and the wind was howling. The troops lost their way. While everybody was worrying, Guan Zhong, the duke's chief minister, suggested: "An old horse may know the way." So the duke ordered several old horses to be selected to lead the army. Finally, they found the way back home.

This idiom refers to the value of experience.

梁上君子

liáng shàng jūnzǐ

A Gentleman on the Beam

东汉(公元25—220)时有个人叫陈寔(shí)。有一天晚上,一个小偷潜入他的房间,躲在房屋梁上,准备等主人睡熟以后下来偷东西。陈寔看见了,把子孙召集起来,大声对他们说:“人应该有志气啊!坏人不是生来就坏,如果做坏事成了习惯,就难于改过来了。房梁上的那位君子就是这样的人!”小偷听见后,连忙跳下来磕(kē)头认罪。

人们借用这个故事,把偷东西的贼称为“梁上君子”。

In the Eastern Han Dynasty (25-220) there was a man called Chen Shi. One night, a thief slipped into his room. Hiding above the beam, the thief waited for Chen Shi to go to sleep. Chen Shi, noticing the thief, called his children and grandchildren together, saying, “To be a man one should have aspirations. Evildoers are not born evil. But if one gets used to doing evil things, it will be hard to reform. The gentleman above the beam is such a man.” The thief, hearing this, hurriedly jumped down and knelt on the ground to beg forgiveness.

This idiom is used to refer to a thief.

临渴掘井

lín kě jué jǐng

Not Digging a Well Until One Is Thirsty

春秋时代，国君鲁昭公在鲁国呆不下去，跑到了齐国。他对齐景公谈起自己过去的错误，感到很后悔。齐景公认为他应该回鲁国去，今后还可能成为一位贤明的国君。而齐国的官员晏子说："已经面临着威胁的人，才急着去铸（zhù）造兵器；吃东西噎（yē）住了咽喉的人，才急着去挖井取水。即使再快，也来不及了。"

"临渴掘井"这个成语比喻事前毫无准备，临到需要时，才急忙想办法。

In the Spring and Autumn Period, Duke Zhao of the State of Lu fled to the State of Qi, following palace turmoil. He admitted his mistakes to Duke Jing of Qi. Duke Jing advised him to go back to Lu, as he might become a wise ruler, since he recognised his faults. But Yanzi, an official of Qi, said, "It is too late to make weapons when one is endangered, and to dig a well when one is choked in eating and needs water desperately."

This idiom warns against not being prepared, but seeking help at the last moment.

满城风雨

mǎn chéng fēngyǔ

A Storm Enveloping the City

北宋时期,有个很会写诗的人,叫潘大临。重阳节快要到了,风雨搅动着秋天的树林,潘大临诗兴大发,提笔写了一句很美的诗:“满城风雨近重阳”。正要往下面写的时候,突然催税的人闯了进来,潘大临就再也没有诗兴往下面写了。

以后人们用“满城风雨”这个成语形容某个消息或事情一经传出,到处议论纷纷。

In the Northern Song Dynasty, there was a man called Pan Dalin who was a renowned poet. As the Double Ninth Festival was approaching, the trees swayed in the autumn wind and rain. The poet, inspired by the scene, wrote a beautiful line: "The Double Ninth Festival is approaching with wind and rain sweeping across the town." Just at this moment, the local tax collector came to demand payment. Thereupon, all Pan's inspiration vanished.

Later, the first part of the line came to be used as a set phrase meaning "the talk of the town".

盲人摸象

máng rén mō xiàng

Blind Men Touching an Elephant

有几个盲人在一起，想知道象究竟是什么东西。有一个摸着象的门牙说:“象像一根大萝卜”;有一个摸着象的耳朵说:“象像一把大扇子”;有一个摸着象的腿说:“象像一根大柱子”;有一个摸着象的身躯说:“象像一堵墙”;有一个摸着象的尾巴说:“象像一条蛇”。他们争论不休,都认为自己说得不错。

“盲人摸象”这个故事用来比喻那些片面观察事物的人,不了解事物的整体或本质。

A group of blind men gathered around an elephant, trying to find out what the creature looked like. One of them happened to touch one of the tusks, and said: “An elephant is just like a turnip.” Another touched one of the elephant's ears, and said, “It is like a big fan.” One put his arms around one of the beast's legs, and said: “It is like a column.” One who happened to place his hands on the body of the elephant said, “It is like a wall.” But the one who got hold of the tail said, “It is like a snake.” They then fell to arguing with each other.

This idiom is used to satirize those who know only part of a thing and not the entirety or essence.

毛遂自荐

Máo Suì zì jiàn

Mao Sui Recommending Himself

战国时代,秦国军队攻打赵国的都城。赵国的平原君打算亲自到楚国去请救兵,想挑选一个精明能干的人一同前去。有一个名叫毛遂的人,自告奋勇愿意同去。平原君到楚国后,与楚王谈了半天,没有一点结果。毛遂怒气冲冲地拿着宝剑,逼近楚王,终于迫使楚王答应出兵,与赵国联合共同抵抗秦国。

"毛遂自荐"这个成语用来比喻自己推荐自己,不必别人介绍。

In the Warring States Period, the State of Qin besieged the capital of the State of Zhao. Duke Pingyuan of Zhao planned to ask the ruler of the State of Chu personally for assistance. He wanted to select a capable man to go with him. A man called Mao Sui volunteered. When the negotiations between the two states were stalled because the ruler of Chu hesitated to send troops, Mao Sui approached him, brandishing a sword. At that, the ruler of Chu agreed to help Zhao, against Qin.

This idiom means to recommend oneself.

门庭若市

mén tíng ruò shì

A Courtyard as Crowded as a Marketplace

战国时代，齐威王接受了大臣邹忌（jì）的建议，决心广泛听取意见，治理国家。于是他发布了一条命令："不管是朝廷的臣子或地方的官吏和百姓，凡能够当面指责我的过失的受上赏；上书规劝我的受中赏；在公共场所议论和批评我的过失、让我知道的受下赏。"命令公布以后，大家纷纷跑到齐威王那里去提意见，王宫的大门口和庭院里热闹得像市场一样。

后来，"门庭若市"变成一个成语，用来形容来往人多，非常热闹的景象。

In the Warring States Period, Duke Wei of the State of Qi accepted the suggestion of his minister Zou Ji and decided to gather widely opinions on ruling the state. He issued an order: "Regardless of whether a man is a minister or a commoner, anyone who points out my faults to my face will get the first prize; anyone who advises me in a memorial will get the second prize; anyone who criticizes me in public will get the third prize." When they learned about this, the people flocked to the duke's palace to present their opinions. The area in front of the palace gate was as busy as a market.

From this story is derived the idiom which describes a very busy scene.

名落孙山

míng luò Sūn Shān

Failing to Pass an Examination

宋朝(公元960—1279)时有一个擅(shàn)长幽默(yōumò)的人,名叫孙山。有一年,他去参加科举考试。榜发出来,孙山考上了最后一名。回到家乡,一位同乡向他打听自己的儿子考上没有。孙山笑了一笑说:“孙山考上最后一名,您儿子的名字还在孙山后面呢。”

后来人们用“名落孙山”来比喻考试没有考上或者选拔没有被录取。

In the Song Dynasty (960-1279) there was a joker called Sun Shan. One year he went to take the imperial examination, and came bottom of the list of successful candidates. Back in his hometown, one of his neighbours asked him whether the neighbour's son had also passed. Sun Shan said, with a smile: "Sun Shan was the last on the list. Your son came after Sun Shan."

Later, people used this idiom to indicate failing in an examination or competition.

南辕北辙

nán yuán běi zhé

Going South by Driving the Chariot North

从前有个人要到南方去，他坐的车子却向北方行驶。过路人说："你去南方，车子怎么向北行驶呢？"他回答说："我的马很能跑路，我的车夫驾车的技术也很高明，加上我又带了充足的路费。"这个人没有考虑到，方向弄反了，他的条件越好，离他要去的地方就越远。

后来人们就把这个故事概括为"南辕北辙"，比喻一个人的行动和他的目的正好相反。

Once a man wanted to go to the south, but his carriage was heading north. A passer-by asked him: "If you are going to the south, why is your chariot heading north?" The man answered, "My horse is good at running, my driver is highly skilled at driving a carriage, and I have enough money." The man didn't consider that the direction might be wrong; the better his conditions were, the further he was away from his destination.

The idiom derived from this story indicates that one's action was the opposite effect to one's intention.

辕：车前驾牲口的木头。

Shafts of a cart.

辙：车轮压出的痕迹，指道路。

The track of a wheel, referring to a road.

怒发冲冠

nù fà chōng guān

So Angry That One's Hair Lifts Up One's Hat

战国时代,赵国的大臣蔺相如出使到秦国。在他向秦王索回玉璧(bì)的时候,秦王蛮(mán)不讲理,蔺相如气愤得连头发都竖了起来,向上冲着帽子。

后来人们用"怒发冲冠"这个成语形容人愤怒到了极点。

In the Warring States Period, Lin Xiangru, chief minister of the State of Zhao, was sent as an envoy to the State of Qin to ask the ruler of Qin to return a fine piece of jade to Zhao. But the ruler of Qin was rude and unreasonable. Lin was angry, and his hair stood up so stiffly on his head that it lifted up his hat.

This idiom came to be used to mean being extremely angry.

披荆斩棘

pī jīng zhǎn jí

Breaking Open a Way Through Brambles and Thorns

东汉的第一个皇帝叫刘秀。在刘秀打天下的时候,冯异立过很多战功,得到刘秀的信任。后来有人借故诬告冯异,刘秀当着大臣的面说:“冯异是我打天下的助手,替我劈开了前进道路上的荆棘(比喻扫除了障碍),我才获得了成功。”

后来人们根据上面的故事,造出“披荆斩棘”这个成语,用来比喻扫除前进道路上的种种障碍,奋勇前进。

The first emperor of the Eastern Han Dynasty, Liu Xiu, greatly trusted a man named Feng Yi, who had helped him attain the throne. When someone slandered Feng Yi, Liu Xiu told his ministers: "Feng Yi helped me to gain power. I succeeded because he broke through the thistles and thorns on the way (removed obstacles)."

The idiom derived from this story means to clear away difficulties and bravely advance.

荆棘:丛生的多刺植物。

Thistles and thorns.

蚍蜉撼树

pífú hàn shù

An Ant Trying to Shake a Big Tree

韩愈是唐朝(618—907)时候著名的文学家。他在一首诗里写过这样两句话:“蚍蜉撼大树,可笑不自量。”蚍蜉是一种大蚂蚁,它自认为力量很大,可以把大树摇动,真是太可笑了。

“蚍蜉撼树”这个成语以后用来比喻力量很小而妄想动摇强大的事物。

Han Yu was a famous poet of the Tang Dynasty (618-907). In one of his poems he wrote, “An ant tries to topple a giant tree, ridiculously overrating its ability.”

This idiom later was used to indicate overestimating one's power and trying to overthrow someone much stronger.

破釜沉舟

pò fǔ chén zhōu

Smashing the Cauldrons and Sinking the Boats

秦朝(公元前221—公元前206)末年,楚霸王项羽率领部队与秦军作战。部队渡过漳河以后,项羽命令士兵把所有的船只都毁掉沉到河底,把行军的饭锅全部打碎,每人只发给三天的粮食。项羽这样做的目的,是向大家表示只能胜利前进、不能失败后退的决心。果然,部队经过九次激烈的战斗,终于打垮了秦军。

“破釜沉舟”这个成语比喻下定最后的决心,不顾一切干到底。

During the late years of the Qin Dynasty (221 - 206 BC), Xiang Yu led a rebellion. After crossing the Zhang River, Xiang Yu ordered his men to sink all their boats and break their cooking pots. He issued each soldier three days' rations and warned them that there was no way to retreat; the only thing they could do to survive was to advance and fight. After nine fierce battles, the Qin army was finally defeated.

This idiom is used to indicate one's firm determination to achieve one's goal at any cost.

釜:古代的锅。

An ancient pot.

破镜重圆

pò jìng chóng yuán

A Broken Mirror Made Whole Again

南朝陈国(公元557—589)将要灭亡的时候,驸马徐德言把一面铜镜破开,跟妻子各留下一半。双方约定:如果将来夫妻失散了,就把它当做信物。后来,夫妻二人真的失散了。凭借着各人留下的半面镜子,他们最终又得到团圆。

"破镜重圆"这个成语比喻夫妻失散或分离后重新团聚。

In the Northern and Southern Dynasties when the State of Chen (557-589) was facing its demise, Xu Deyan, husband of the princess, broke a bronze mirror into halves. Each of them kept a half as tokens in case they were separated. Soon afterwards, they did lose touch with each other, but the two halves of the mirror enabled them to be reunited.

This idiom is used to refer to the reunion of a couple after they lose touch or break up.

骑虎难下

qí hǔ nán xià

When One Rides a Tiger It Is Hard to Dismount

北周最后一个皇帝年龄很小，大臣杨坚掌握了国家大权。杨坚的妻子劝告杨坚说："北周已经不行了。你现在就像骑在老虎背上，形势逼迫着你不能下来，只好干下去吧！"杨坚觉得很有道理，后来就自己当了皇帝，建立了隋朝(公元581—618)，并且统一了中国。

"骑虎难下"这个成语用来比喻做事中途遇到很大困难，但形势所迫，又不能中止。

Yang Jian was the regent of the last king of Northern Zhou (557-581). His wife advised him: "Northern Zhou is dying. Now it is as if you are riding on the back of a tiger: It will be dangerous to dismount. You can do nothing but continue." Yang thought this quite reasonable. Later, he founded the Sui Dynasty, and united China once more.

This idiom is used as a metaphor meaning that one is in a difficult situation and cannot help but continue to pursue one's course.

杞人忧天

Qǐ rén yōu tiān

The Man of Qi Who Worried That the Sky Would Fall

春秋时代,杞国有一个喜欢胡思乱想的人。一天,他竟然想到,天会塌下来,地会陷下去,自己到哪里去安身?这个人越想越害怕,整天愁眉苦脸,坐立不安,白天吃不下饭,晚上睡不着觉。后来有人耐心地开导他,他才放下了心。

"杞人忧天"这个成语讥笑那些没有必要或毫无根据的忧虑。

In the Spring and Autumn Period, in the State of Qi there was a man who always let his imagination run away with him. One day he even worried that the sky would fall on his head. He was so worried that he could neither eat nor sleep. Later, someone persuaded him that his fears were groundless.

This idiom satirizes those who worry unnecessarily.

黔驴技穷

Qián lǘ jì qióng

The Guizhou Donkey Has Exhausted Its Tricks

从前，贵州没有驴子。有人从外地带回一头驴子，拴在山下。一只老虎看到了，以为是什么怪物，急忙躲到树林中去偷偷地瞧。驴子大叫一声，老虎吓了一跳，以为驴子要吃掉自己。时间一长，老虎觉得驴子并没有什么恶意，逐渐走近去戏弄它，触犯它。驴子生气了，用蹄子踢老虎。老虎心里想："你的本领不过就是如此啊！"于是立即扑过去，一口把它咬死吃掉了。

"黔驴技穷"这个成语比喻仅有的一点本事也用完了，再没有别的办法了。

In ancient times there were no donkeys in Guizhou Province. Somebody brought a donkey from somewhere and tied it to a tree at the foot of a mountain. A tiger saw the donkey, and thought that it must be a fearsome monster. It hid behind a tree and spied on the donkey. When the donkey brayed, the tiger was frightened, thinking that the donkey was about to devour it. After a while, seeing that the donkey had not moved, the tiger approached it and teased it. The donkey became angry, and kicked the tiger. The tiger thought to itself: "Is that all it is capable of?" It then jumped on the donkey and ate it.

This idiom is used to mean that one has exhausted one's skills.

黔:贵州省的别称。

Another name for Guizhou Province.

日暮途穷

rì mù tú qióng

The Day Is Waning and the Road Is Ending

春秋时代,楚平王听信谗(chán)言,杀了伍子胥(xū)的父亲。伍子胥逃到吴国,十多年后帮助吴王打到楚国的都城,报了仇。伍子胥虽然报了仇,但是受到国人的责备。伍子胥内心十分痛苦,说:“我就像一个行路的人,天已经晚了,而路途还十分遥远,不知该怎么办啊!”

这个故事后来变成成语“日暮途穷”,比喻处境十分困难,力量用尽了,计策没有了。

In the Spring and Autumn Period, Duke Ping of Chu was misled by slanderers, and had Wu Zixu's father executed. Wu Zixu fled to the State of Wu. More than ten years later, Wu Zixu took his revenge by helping Wu conquer Chu. Yet he suffered agonies of remorse, because his countrymen called him a traitor. He protested, "I'm just like a traveller. It's already late, but I still have a long way to go. I simply don't know what to do."

This idiom comes from the above story. It means being in a very difficult situation, at the end of one's tether.

日暮:天色晚了。

Late in the day.

途穷:路到头了。

To come to the end of a road.

如火如荼

rú huǒ rú tú

Like a Raging Fire

春秋时代，吴王夫差想做几个小国的霸主，率领三万军队向晋军挑战。他命令将士们以一万人为单位摆成一个正方形的阵势。当中的都穿白色衣服，拿着白色的旗帜，远远望去就像遍地盛开着白色荼花。左边的穿红色衣服，拿着红色的旗帜，远远望去就像满山燃烧着熊熊火焰。右边的穿黑色衣服，拿着黑色的旗帜，远远望去像是满天结集着浓密的乌云。夫差想利用这种声势去压倒对方。

“如火如荼”这个成语形容气势旺盛、场面热烈的景象。

During the Spring and Autumn Period, Duke Fuchai of Wu led a huge army against the State of Jin. He ordered his men to form three square contingents. The middle one was dressed in white and holding white flags, which looked from a distance just like the flowers of a field full of reeds. The left unit was in red and holding red flags, which looked from afar like flaming fire all over the mountains. The right unit was in black and holding black flags, which looked from a distance like thick black clouds covering the sky. Fuchai was trying to present to the enemy a show of overwhelming force.

This idiom describes a scene of great momentum and exuberance.

荼:开白花的茅草。

A kind of reed with white tufts.

如鱼得水

rú yú dé shuǐ

To Feel Just like a Fish in Water

三国时代，刘备为了夺得天下，曾经三次到湖北隆中请诸葛(gě)亮出来，辅佐自己。诸葛亮出来以后，协助刘备处理军政大事，得到刘备的高度信任，两人感情越来越好。刘备对手下人说："我有了孔明(诸葛亮的'字')，就好像鱼儿有了水一样。"

"如鱼得水"这个成语比喻得到了和自己非常投合的人，或所处环境对自己非常适合。

In the Three Kingdoms Period, Liu Bei went to Longzhong in Hubei Province three times to ask Zhuge Liang to assist him. Finally, Zhuge Liang helped Liu Bei deal with military affairs and politics, and was greatly trusted by the latter. Their regard for each other became deeper and deeper. Liu Bei said to his ministers: "Having Kong Ming (another name of Zhuge Liang) assist me, I feel just like a stranded fish which has been put back in the water."

This idiom is used to describe finding a boon companion or an ideal situation.

入木三分

rù mù sān fēn

To Enter Three-Tenths of an Inch into the Timber

东晋时代的王羲（xī）之，是中国杰出的书法家。他的字写得既秀丽，又苍劲有力。他平时勤学苦练，即使休息时间也在揣摩（chuǎimó）字体的结构，手不停地在衣服上画。时间长了，衣服都画破了。传说有一次他在木板上写字，刻字的人惊奇地发现，他所写的字，墨汁透入木板竟有三分深！

"入木三分"原本形容王羲之的书法很有功力。后来比喻分析问题十分深刻。

Wang Xizhi was a famous calligrapher of the Eastern Jin Dynasty (317-420). His style was beautiful, bold and vigorous. He was very diligent about practising; even when resting, he would engage in figuring out the structure of characters by "writing" on his clothes unceasingly. With the passage of time, his clothes were worn out by rubbing. It is said that once a carpenter found that the ink of the characters he had written on a plank had soaked almost one centimeter into it.

This idiom originally described the vigour of Wang Xizhi's handwriting. Later it came to be used to mean penetrating analysis.

塞翁失马

sài wēng shī mǎ

The Old Man of the Frontier Lost His Horse

古时候,边塞上有个老人丢了一匹马。邻居知道了,怕他过于悲伤,特地前来安慰他。老人却说:“丢了马本来是一件坏事,但是怎么能知道它不会变成一件好事呢?”过了几个月,丢失的那匹马竟然带着一匹骏马跑了回来。

“塞翁失马”这个成语比喻暂时的损失或挫折,也许因此会得到好处。或者说,坏事在一定条件下可以变成好事。

In ancient times, an old man living on the frontier lost a horse. His neighbour came to comfort him. But the old man said, "Losing a horse could be a bad thing, but it might turn into a good thing. Who can tell?" A few months later, the lost horse came back, bringing with it another fine steed.

This idiom is used metaphorically to mean that sometimes people may benefit from a temporary loss or setback. In other words, a calamity may turn into a blessing.

三顾茅庐

sān gù máolú

Paying Three Visits to the Cottage

三国时，诸葛亮居住在隆中的茅庐里，刘备听说诸葛亮很有学识，又有才能，就带着礼物去请他出来辅助自己打天下。刘备一共去了三次，最后才见到诸葛亮。诸葛亮见刘备十分诚恳，终于答应了他的请求。从此，诸葛亮用全部精力辅助刘备，在军事上和政治上取得了巨大的胜利。

“三顾茅庐”这个成语用来比喻诚心诚意地一再邀请人家。

In the Three Kingdoms Period, Zhuge Liang lived in seclusion in a thatched cottage. Liu Bei, hearing that Zhuge Liang was very knowledgeable and capable, went to visit him, taking gifts, hoping that Zhuge Liang would agree to assist him with statecraft. He had to make three visits before Zhuge Liang agreed to do so, impressed by his sincerity. From then on, Zhuge Liang helped Liu Bei with all his heart, and made great achievements in both the military and political spheres.

This idiom means persisting with sincerity.

顾：拜访。

To visit.

茅庐：草屋。

Thatched cottage.

三人成虎

sān rén chéng hǔ

Repeat a Lie Enough Times and It Will Be Believed

战国时代，魏王的臣子庞（Páng）葱问魏王："现在有一个人说街上有老虎，你相信吗？"魏王说："不相信。"庞葱又问："两个人说街上有老虎，你相信吗？"魏王表示有点怀疑。庞葱又问："三个人说街上有老虎，你相信吗？"魏王说："我相信了。"庞葱说："街上没有老虎是很明显的事，然而三个人都说有老虎你就相信了。要警惕谣言变成真话呀！"

"三人成虎"比喻谣言多次流传，就可能使人信以为真。

In the Warring States Period, Pang Cong, a minister of the State of Wei, said to the ruler of Wei: "Someone said that there are tigers in the streets. Do you believe it?" His master answered, "No, I don't believe it." Pang Cong said later: "Now two people have said that there are tigers in the streets. Do you believe it?" The ruler showed some doubt. Then Pang Cong said again: "Now three people have said the same thing. Do you believe it?" The ruler said, "Yes, I do." Pang Cong continued, "There are no tigers in the streets at all. Yet if three people say the same thing, you believe it! We must be alert against rumours gaining credence."

This idiom points out that a rumour, if repeated often enough, may come to be believed.

丧家之犬

sàng jiā zhī quǎn

A Homeless Dog

春秋时代，孔子带着弟子们周游列国，到处游说，可是四处碰壁。一次走到郑国，与弟子们走散了。孔子站在东城门外，一个人孤零零的。有一个郑国人看到后，讥笑孔子说："看他那副样子，真像一条丧家之犬！"孔子听见后笑了笑，不在意地说："是啊，是啊，真是有点像啊！"

"丧家之犬"本意是指办丧事人家的狗，后来转指无家可归的狗。比喻失去依靠、无处投奔的人。

In the Warring States Period, Confucius led his disciples on visits to various states. They went offering their services everywhere, but were always rebuffed. One day, in the State of Zheng, Confucius lost his disciples. He stood outside the east gate by himself, not knowing what to do. A citizen of Zheng then mocked Confucius: "Look at him," he said. "Isn't he like a stray cur?" Hearing this, Confucius smiled, and said uncaringly: "Yes, yes, indeed."

This idiom originally referred to dogs of families in mourning. Later it came to be used to indicate homeless dogs, and refers metaphorically to people with nowhere to go and no one to turn to.

杀鸡吓猴

shā jī xià hóu

Killing the Chicken to Frighten the Monkeys

古时候，有一个人养了许多猴子。猴子长大后，变得越来越调皮，常常不听主人的话，还弄坏主人的东西，主人很生气。一天，主人捉来一只公鸡，把猴子们叫到跟前，对它们说："你们若是再捣乱，不听话，就像这只鸡一样。"说着，就当着猴子们的面把公鸡杀了。猴子们见到血淋淋的公鸡，非常害怕，以后就变得老实多了。

"杀鸡吓猴"比喻惩罚一个人来吓唬另外一个人或一些人。

In ancient times, there was a man who raised monkeys, which became more and more mischievous as they grew up and often destroyed his things. One day the man caught a cock. He assembled the monkeys and said to them: "If you don't behave and stop causing trouble, you will end up like the cock." Then he killed the cock in front of the monkeys. Seeing this, the monkeys were frightened, and became obedient thereafter.

This idiom is used metaphorically to mean to frighten somebody by punishing someone else.

甚嚣尘上

shèn xiāo chén shàng

Making a Great Clamor

战国时代,晋国和楚国交战。楚共王站在架有高台的战车上观察晋军的动静。看了一会儿,楚王说:“那边人声十分喧嚣,而且尘土都飞扬起来了!”部下说:“这是他们在填井平灶,摆开阵势要作战啦!”

“甚嚣尘上”这个成语,现在比喻对传闻的事情议论纷纷。

Once in the Warring States Period, the State of Jin was at war with the State of Chu. Duke Gong of Chu stood on a high platform built on a chariot and watched the movements of the Jin army. After watching for a while, he said, “It's quite noisy over there and cloud of dust has been stirred up.” His aide answered, “The enemy are filling up wells and destroying their cooking stoves. They are preparing to fight.”

This idiom is now used to mean a lot of commotion over hearsay.

甚:很,极。

Extremely.

嚣:喧闹。

Noise, bustle.

势如破竹

shì rú pò zhú

Like Splitting Bamboo

晋朝时候，大将军杜预带兵攻打吴国，一路上打了很多胜仗。有人认为应该暂时休整一下，第二年再继续进攻。杜预说："现在我们的士气正旺盛，攻打吴国就象劈竹子一样，等到劈开几节之后，下面的就会迎刃而解了。" 后来杜预果然灭掉了吴国。

"势如破竹" 这个成语比喻作战或工作节节胜利，势不可挡。另一个成语"迎刃而解"比喻主要问题解决了，其它有关问题就可以顺利地解决。

In the Jin Dynasty (265-420), General Du Yu led troops to attack the State of Wu. He achieved victory after victory along the route. Somebody suggested that they should stop and take a rest until the following year. But Du Yu said, "Now the morale of our troops is very high. Attacking Wu is just like splitting a bamboo: Having split open the first few joints, the rest will be easily split." So he went on to eliminate the State of Wu.

This idiom means winning a victory with irresistible force. Another idiom, 迎刃而解, means that if the major problem is solved, other relevant problems will be settled easily.

世外桃源

shì wài Táoyuán

A Haven of Peace and Happiness

东晋的文学家陶渊明写了一篇著名的文章叫《桃花源记》。叙述一个渔人出外捕鱼的时候,偶然来到了桃花源这个地方。从这里通过一个山洞,发现了一个村子，这里的居民是秦朝时避难人的后代。这是一个与世隔绝、没有剥削和压迫、人人安居乐业的美好社会。渔人告别村民回家以后,再也找不到这个地方了。

后来,由这个故事产生了"世外桃源"这个成语,用来比喻与世隔绝的、理想的美好世界。

Tao Yuanming, a famous writer of the Eastern Jin Dynasty (317-420), wrote the well-known essay *Peach-Blossom Spring*. In it he tells a story which goes like this: A fisherman happened to come upon a place called Peach-Blossom Spring. Squeezing through a cave, he found a village, the residents of which were descendants of refugees from the Qin Dynasty. It was a paradise isolated from the outside world, without exploitation or oppression, and everybody living and working in peace and contentment. The fisherman left the villagers and went home. But he could never find the place again.

This idiom is derived from the above story, and is used to mean an isolated, ideal world.

手不释卷

shǒu bù shì juàn

Always with a Book in Hand

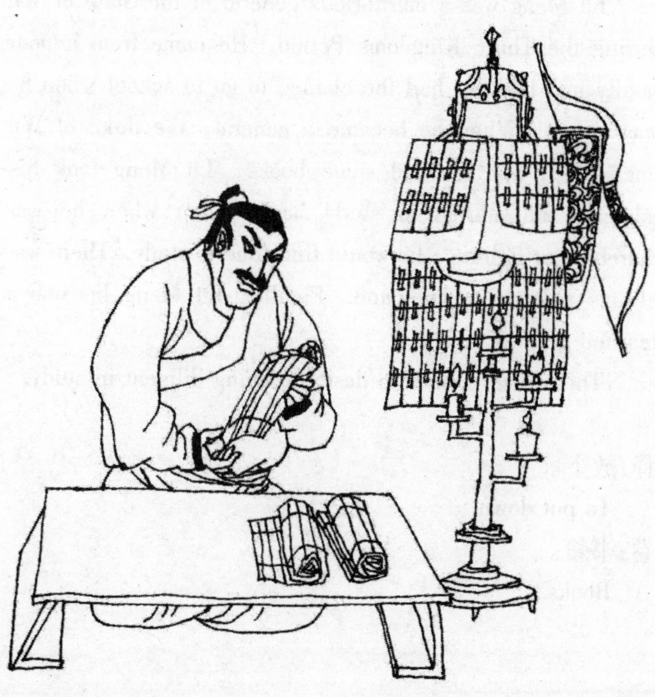

吕蒙是三国时代吴国的一员大将，曾经立过不少战功。但由于小时候家境贫苦，没能上学读书。他当了大将以后，国王孙权鼓励他要多读书。吕蒙听从了孙权的建议，每天坚持不懈、专心致志地读书，哪怕是在行军作战的紧张时刻，也挤出时间来学习，手里总是不丢开书本。后来吕蒙终于成为一名学识渊博的将军。

“手不释卷”这个成语形容人学习十分用功。

Lü Meng was a meritorious general of the State of Wu during the Three Kingdoms Period. He came from a poor family and had not had the chance to go to school when he was young. When he became a general, the duke of Wu encouraged him to read some books. Lü Meng took his advice, and started to study hard. Even when he was marching or fighting, he would find time to study. There was always a book in his hand. Finally, Lü Meng became a learned general.

This idiom is used to describe being diligent in study.

释:放下。

To put down.

卷:书籍。

Books.

守株待兔

shǒu zhū dài tù

Sitting by a Stump, Waiting for a Careless Hare

春秋时代，宋国有个农夫，一天在耕田的时候，忽然跑来一只兔子，恰巧碰在树桩上，脖子折断死了。农夫把兔子拾回家去，美美地吃了一顿兔肉。晚上他想："我何必辛辛苦苦地种地呢？每天在树下能捡到一只兔子就够我吃的了。"于是，他从此不再耕作，每天坐在树下等待兔子的到来。

"守株待兔"这个成语，讥笑那些不想经过努力，存在侥幸心理，希望得到意外收获的人。

In the Spring and Autumn Period, a farmer in the State of Song was one day working in the fields, when he saw a rabbit bump into a tree stump accidentally and break its neck. The farmer took the rabbit home, and cooked himself a delicious meal. That night he thought, "I needn't work so hard. All I have to do is wait for a rabbit each day by the stump." So from then on he gave up farming, and simply sat by the stump waiting for rabbits to come and run into it.

This idiom satirizes those who just wait for a stroke of luck, rather than making efforts to obtain what they need.

株：树桩。

Tree stump.

蜀犬吠日

Shǔ quǎn fèi rì

A Sichuan Dog Barks at the Sun

唐朝（公元618—907）著名的文学家柳宗元，曾经讲过一个“蜀犬吠日”的故事。在中国西南地区的四川省，那里的气候多雨多雾，有时阴雨连绵、雾气蒙蒙长达数月，一年四季很难看见太阳。所以那里的狗一见到太阳出来，都感到很新奇，就大声狂叫起来。

“蜀犬吠日”这个成语比喻少见多怪（对本来是很平常的事情，由于见识短浅而感到奇怪）。

A leading writer of the Tang Dynasty (618-907), Liu Zongyuan, related how in Sichuan Province in southwest China it was cloudy and foggy most of the year. The sun was hardly ever seen. So if the sun came out, the local dogs would feel that something strange was happening, and bark loudly.

This idiom is used to indicate being surprised at something normal, due to one's ignorance.

蜀：四川省的别称。

Another name for Sichuan Province.

吠：狗叫。

To bark.

束之高阁

shù zhī gāo gé

Putting It on a High Shelf

晋朝(265—420)时候有个叫殷(Yīn)浩的人,很有才能,又善于辩论,后来当了将军。可是在一次战争中打了败仗,被免了官,在家闲着。有人建议请殷浩再次出来做官。另一个叫做庾(Yǔ)翼的将军听见了,不同意这个建议。他对人说:"像殷浩这样的人,只应该把他捆起来放到高高的架子上,等天下太平了,再请他出来做官吧。"

后来人们就用"束之高阁"这个成语比喻把某人、某种东西或某件事物扔在一边,不去利用它。

In the Jin Dynasty (265-420), there was a man called Yin Hao who was both capable and eloquent. Failure in a battle caused him to lose his position as a general. Someone suggested assigning Yin Hao again. But a general called Yu Yi did not agree, saying, "All we can do with someone like Yin Hao is tie him up and put him on a high shelf. We should not assign him again until the country is at peace."

Later this idiom was used to mean putting aside something or someone and ignore it or him.

束:捆。

To tie up.

水落石出

shuǐ luò shí chū

When the Water Ebbs, Stones Will Appear

北宋时代的大文学家苏东坡，贬（biǎn）官到了湖北黄州。他两次到黄州赤壁游览，写下了著名的《前赤壁赋》和《后赤壁赋》。在后面一篇文章中，有“山高月小，水落石出”的著名句子。其中“水落石出”描述了长江的景象：江水下落，原来被淹没在水下面的石头有的就显露出来了。

“水落石出”这个成语用来比喻经过反复调查以后，事实的真相终于彻底弄明白了。

In the Northern Song Dynasty (960-1127), the poet Su Dongpo was once banished to Huangzhou in Hubei Province. There he visited the Red Cliff twice and wrote prose pieces called *The First Visit to the Red Cliff* and *The Second Visit to the Red Cliff*. In the latter work, there is a line which goes: "High mountains and small moon, the rocks emerge when the water subsides."

This idiom is used metaphorically to mean that the whole comes to light after repeated investigation.

四面楚歌

sì miàn Chǔ gē

Songs of Chu on All Sides

秦朝末年,楚和汉争夺天下。楚王项羽被汉王刘邦的军队紧紧地围困在垓(Gāi)下这个地方。项羽的兵士已经很少,粮食也没有了,危急万分。夜里,四面包围着的汉军唱起了楚地的民歌。项羽听了,非常吃惊地说:“汉军已经全部占领了楚国的土地吗?为什么在汉军中有这么多的人会唱楚歌呢?”说着就从床上爬起来,带着残余的士兵惊慌地逃走了。

“四面楚歌”这个成语比喻四面受到敌人的攻击,处于孤立危急的困境。

At the end of the Qin Dynasty (221-206 BC), the State of Chu and the State of Han fought for control of the country. Xiang Yu, the king of Chu, was besieged at a place called Gaixia by the Han army led by Liu Bang. Xiang Yu was in a desperate situation, with little food and only a few soldiers. At night, the surrounding Han troops started to sing Chu folk songs. Xiang Yu was very surprised at this, and said, “Has Liu Bang occupied the whole of Chu? How can he have drafted so many Chu people into his army?” Then he fled together with the remainder of his forces.

This idiom is used metaphorically to mean to be in a helpless and critical situation, surrounded by the enemy on all sides.

谈虎色变

tán hǔ sè biàn

Turn Pale at the Mention of a Tiger

从前有一个人给大家讲老虎伤人的故事，讲得有声有色，周围的人都听得津津有味。其中有个农夫，有一次在山上砍柴时曾被一只老虎咬伤，差一点送了命。所以这个农夫听了老虎的故事，尤其感到害怕，脸的颜色都改变了。

“谈虎色变”这个成语比喻一提到可怕的事情，就表现出非常紧张、恐怖的样子。

Once upon a time, a man was telling stories about how tigers can injure people. Among the listeners there was a farmer who had once been attacked by a tiger and almost lost his life. He was so scared that his face turned pale.

This idiom means looking nervous and fearful when something awful is mentioned.

昙花一现

tánhuā yī xiàn

A Flower That Vanishes as Soon as It Appears

昙花是一种美丽而珍贵的花。这种花多在夜间开放，开花的时间又极短，很快就凋谢了。所以人们很难得看见。按照佛教的传说，转轮王出世，昙花才能生长出来，极力形容昙花难得出现。

“昙花一现”比喻事物或人物出现不久就消失了。

The broad-leaved epiphyllum is a beautiful and precious white flower which usually blooms at night, and its blossom only lasts for a brief period. According to a Buddhist legend, the plant blooms only on the birth of divine kings.

This idiom describes things which disappear shortly after they come into being.

螳臂当车

tánɡ bì dānɡ chē

A Mantis Trying to Halt a Chariot

这是一则寓言。

从前有一个车夫,驾着马车在路上行驶。忽然前面跳来一只螳螂,举起镰刀一样的前腿,恶狠狠地挡住车轮的前进。车夫没有理会它,车轮就从螳螂的身上压了过去。

"螳臂当车"这个成语比喻不估计自己的力量,去做办不到的事情,必然要遭到失败。也说"螳臂挡车"。

Once a carter was driving his cart, when a mantis jumped out in front of the cart. Raising its forelegs, it tried to obstruct the passage of the cart. Of course, it was crushed by one of the wheels.

This idiom is used to mean overrating oneself and trying to do what is beyond one's ability. The result can be nothing but failure. It also appears as 螳臂挡车.

当:阻挡。

To obstruct.

天花乱坠

tiān huā luàn zhuì

As If It Were Raining Flowers

南北朝梁武帝的时候，有一个名叫云光的法师，讲经讲得很好。传说他有一次登坛(tán)讲经，感动了天上的花神。花神把天上的花纷纷降落下来，洒遍了大地。

“天花乱坠”这个成语后来比喻说话有声有色，非常动听(多指夸大的或不切实际的讲话)。

In the Southern and Northern Dynasties (420-589), in the reign of King Wu of Liang, there was a monk called Master Yun Guang who was a very accomplished preacher. Once he explained the sutra so profoundly and subtly that the God of Flowers was moved and sent divine flowers down to Earth. Soon the land was covered with flowers.

This idiom was later used metaphorically to describe talking in a vivid and eloquent way (mostly in an exaggerated and impractical manner).

天涯海角

tiān yá hǎi jiǎo

The End of the Sky and the Corner of the Sea

天的边缘(天涯),海的角落(海角),都是指非常遥远的地方。位于中国最南端的海南岛,自古以来被人们认为是“天涯海角”。北宋时代的大文学家苏轼,晚年被贬官来到这个地方。传说海南岛最南面巨石上的“天涯”两个字,就是苏轼写的。

这个成语用来形容极远的地方，或者两个人彼此相隔遥远。

The “edge of heaven and the corner of the sea” both refer to the remotest place. Hainan Island, located in the southernmost part of China, was considered the remotest place in ancient times. Su Shi, a famous poet of the Northern Song Dynasty, was exiled there in his later years. It is said that the two characters 天涯 on a huge rock on the southernmost tip of the island were written by Su Shi.

This idiom refers to the remotest places or a very long distance between two people.

天衣无缝

tiān yī wú fèng

Divine Garments Without Seams

唐朝有个人叫郭翰(hàn)。一个夏天的晚上，月光非常明亮。他忽然看见天空中有个女子轻盈而缓慢地飘落下来。他仔细地观察那个女子，发现她身上穿的衣服连一条缝（fèng）也没有，感到非常奇怪，便问那个女子。女子回答说："天衣本来就用不着针线缝(féng)合的呀!"

"天衣无缝"这个成语用来比喻处理事情十分周密，不露一点痕迹。也比喻诗文写得很精辟，找不出一点毛病。

There was a man called Guo Han in the Tang Dynasty (618-907). One summer night, when the moon was very bright, he suddenly saw a girl descending slowly from the sky. He observed the girl closely, and found that the dress she was wearing was seamless. He was puzzled, and asked why. The girl answered, "Heavenly clothes are not sewn with needle and thread."

This idiom is used metaphorically to indicate the flawless handling of things. It can also be used to indicate a perfectly written poem or other literary article.

同舟共济

tóng zhōu gòng jì

Crossing a River in the Same Boat

春秋时代，吴国人和越国人经常相互打仗，成为仇敌。一次，河水泛滥，两国的人同乘一条船打算过河。船到河中间，遇到了大风，情况十分危急。两国人不分彼此，不再争斗，而是互相帮助，终于安全地渡过了河。

“同舟共济”这个成语比喻在遇到困难的时候，大家同心协力共同渡过难关。

In the Spring and Autumn Period, the State of Wu and the State of Yue often fought with each other, and their peoples looked upon each other as enemies. Once, people from the two states were crossing a river in the same boat. When the boat was in the middle of the river, a strong wind threatened to sink it. The people from the two states cooperated to ensure the safe arrival of the boat.

This idiom indicates that people should pull together to overcome difficulties, burying their differences in a time of common danger.

济:过河。

To cross a river.

偷天换日

tōu tiān huàn rì

Stealing the Sky and Changing the Sun

广阔无边的天空能够把它偷走吗？光芒四射的太阳能够把它换掉吗？偏偏就有那么一种人，妄想玩弄手法，偷走天空，换掉太阳。

“偷天换日”这个成语，用夸张的语言，比喻暗中玩弄手法，改变重大事物的真相来欺骗别人。

Can the boundless sky be stolen? Can the radiant sun be changed? There are certain people who are so keen on playing tricks that they even want to steal the sky and change the sun.

This idiom uses exaggerated words to indicate perpetrating fraud by changing important facts secretly.

图穷匕见

tú qióng bǐ xiàn

When the Map Is Unrolled the Dagger Is Revealed

战国末年，有一个武士荆轲受燕国太子的托付去刺杀秦王。为了能够接近秦王,荆轲便以向秦王奉献地图为名，预先把刺人的匕首藏在地图里面。秦王慢慢地展开地图,到了最后,藏在地图里的匕首就露了出来。

“图穷匕见”比喻事情发展到最后阶段，真相或本意终于暴露出来。

In the late years of the Warring States Period, Jing Ke was entrusted by the crown prince of the State of Yan to assassinate the ruler of the State of Qin. In order to be able to get close to the latter, Jing Ke pretended to want to present to him a valuable map. The assassin had hidden a dagger in the rolled-up map. When the map was unrolled, the dagger was revealed.

This idiom means that when things come to the final stage, the truth or the real intention is revealed.

见:同现,表露在外面。

Same as 现, being exposed.

完璧归赵

wán bì guī Zhào

Returning the Jade Intact to Zhao

战国时代，秦王听说赵王有一块无价之宝的“和氏璧”，就写信给赵王，愿意拿十五座城来交换这块玉璧。赵王派大臣蔺相如到秦国去送玉璧。相如把玉璧献给秦王后，秦王却不打算把十五座城让给赵国。相如看破了秦王的花招，就用一个巧妙的计策把秦王骗去的玉璧弄了回来，并悄悄派人送回了赵国。

“完璧归赵”这个成语比喻借了别人的东西能够完整无损地归还给原主。

In the Warring States Period, the ruler of Qin heard that the ruler of Zhao had a piece of priceless jade. So he offered 15 cities in exchange for it. At this, the ruler of Zhao sent his minister Lin Xiangru with the jade to the State of Qin. But after presenting the jade to the ruler of Qin, Lin Xiangru sensed a trick. By a ruse he managed to get the jade back, and then threatened to smash it against a pillar. Rather than see the jade destroyed, the ruler of Qin allowed Lin to keep it for a few days before a formal handover ceremony. Then Lin Xiangru secretly had it sent back to his state intact.

This idiom now means returning what one has borrowed intact to the owner.

璧:古代的一种玉器。

A round flat piece of jade with a hole in the center.

亡羊补牢

wáng yáng bǔ láo

Mending the Fold After the Sheep Have Been Stolen

从前有个人养了许多羊,有一次,他的羊圈破了一个口子,没有引起他的注意。过了几天他发现少了好几只羊，这时才后悔得不得了。邻人劝他说:“羊已经丢失了，现在把羊圈赶快修补起来还不算晚啊!”

“亡羊补牢”这个成语比喻在受到损失以后，如果及时想办法补救,可以避免更大的损失。

A man who raised sheep once noticed that there was a hole in the wall of his sheepfold. But he neglected to repair it. A few days later, several sheep were missing. His neighbour advised him: “It is not too late to mend the sheepfold.”

This idiom advises us that even though we have suffered a loss, it is never too late to take steps to prevent further losses.

亡:丢失。

To lose.

牢:养牲畜的圈。

Pen, fold.

望梅止渴

wàng méi zhǐ kě

Looking at Plums to Quench the Thirst

三国时代,有一次曹操带领军队去打仗。在行军的路上,找不到水源,士兵们都感到口渴难忍。曹操想出一个计策,指着前面一片树林说:“那里就是一大片梅林,树上的梅子又甜又酸,可以解渴。”士兵们听了,想起梅子的酸味,一个个都流出了口水,再也不觉得口渴了。

“望梅止渴”这个成语比喻用空想来安慰自己。

In the Three Kingdoms Period (220-280), Cao Cao was once on a campaign during which his men failed to find any water. Cao Cao told them: “There are plum trees ahead. The sweet and sour plums will relieve your thirst.” Hearing this, the soldiers thought of the plums, and their mouths watered. This cured their thirst.

This idiom means to comfort oneself with fantasy.

望洋兴叹

wàng yáng xīng tàn

Gazing at the Ocean and Sighing

有一年秋天,河里发了大水,河水淹没了田地和树林,到处都是白茫茫的一片。河神看到这种景象,自以为很伟大,很了不起。他顺着河水来到了北海,望见海洋无边无际,水几乎和天空连在一起,这时他才感叹起来,觉得自己真是太渺小了。

“望洋兴叹”原来的意思是:看到人家的伟大,才感到自己很渺小。现在多用来比喻做事力量不够,无从着手,而感到无可奈何。

One autumn, the rivers flooded, leaving a vast expanse of water everywhere. Seeing this, the god of the rivers was filled with pride at his vast domain. He then journeyed to the Northern Sea. When he saw the mighty ocean stretching to the horizon, he realized how puny he actually was, and sighed with disappointment.

This idiom originally meant feeling one's own insignificance upon seeing another's might. Now it is mostly used to indicate being able to do nothing but sigh in the face of a huge task.

为虎作伥

wèi hǔ zuò chāng

Helping the Tiger to Pounce upon Its Victims

古代有个奇怪的传说：有一只老虎把人咬死以后，吃掉人身上的肉，却不让他的灵魂离开。这个灵魂下次还要帮着老虎去吃人，这样的人叫伥鬼。伥鬼带着老虎去寻找第二个人，让老虎再把那个人咬死、吃掉，这时伥鬼才能够获得自由。

这个可笑的传说，后来就变成了“为虎作伥”这个成语，用来比喻替恶人做帮凶，引诱或帮助恶人干坏事。

An ancient legend has it that a tiger ate a man, and the man's soul could not be freed until it found another man for the tiger to eat.

This idiom means to do evil things in the service of the wicked.

卧薪尝胆

wò xīn cháng dǎn

Sleeping on Brushwood and Tasting Gall

春秋时代,越国被吴国打败了。越王勾践和他的妻子都被带到吴国做苦工。后来勾践被放回越国,他立志要报亡国之仇。从此,他每天夜里睡在柴草上面,不用被褥。在他住的地方,悬挂着一个苦胆,吃饭和睡觉以前,都要尝一尝苦胆的味道,以提醒自己不忘过去的耻辱。经过十年的艰苦奋斗,越国终于战胜了吴国。

"卧薪尝胆"这个成语用来形容刻苦自励,奋发图强。

In the Spring and Autumn Period, the State of Wu defeated the State of Yue, and took the king of Yue, Gou Jian, and his wife prisoner. For several years, Gou Jian laboured as a slave in Wu. When he was released and returned to Yue, Gou Jian was determined to take revenge for losing his state. So that he would never forget his humiliation, he slept on a pile of brushwood and tasted gall before every meal. After ten years of careful preparations, he attacked and finally conquered the State of Wu.

This idiom is used to describe inspiring oneself and working hard to accomplish an ambition.

薪:柴草。

Brushwood.

笑里藏刀

xiào lǐ cáng dāo

Hiding a Dagger Behind a Smile

唐朝有一个大臣李义府，表面上对人温和恭顺，跟人谈话总是面带微笑。但是，内心深处却十分阴险毒辣。凡是能力比他强的人，他都要设法加以打击和谋害。当时人们称他是“笑中刀”。

“笑里藏刀”是由“笑中刀”转化而来的，比喻表面装得善良和气，而内心暗藏阴险毒辣。

In the Tang Dynasty, there was a minister called Li Yifu who was always affable and smiling. But in his heart he was very sinister and ruthless. He constantly schemed against people he saw as possible rivals. He was called “The knife in the smile”.

This idiom, derived from the above story, means disguising a ruthless nature behind a pleasant appearance.

胸有成竹

xiōng yǒu chéng zhú

Having a Ready-Formed Plan

宋朝画家文同，特别喜欢画竹子。他在园子里种了许多竹子，经常仔细观察竹子的生长过程，特别是在晴天、雨后以及春夏秋冬不同季节下竹子的各种形态，对竹子有了较深切的了解。一旦到他提笔绘画时，他的胸中早已有了竹子的形象，所以总是能够把竹子画得生动逼真，活灵活现。

“胸有成竹”用来比喻在做事情以前，已经有了充分成熟的考虑，因而成功的把握很大。

In the Song Dynasty, an artist called Wen Tong was especially fond of drawing bamboos. He planted a lot of bamboos in his garden so that he could observe the process of their growth and appearance in different seasons. He knew bamboos so well that whenever he took up the paintbrush he already had a picture in his mind, and thus he could always paint bamboos in a vivid and lively way.

This idiom is used to indicate having a well-thought-out plan already before one sets out to do something, making success assured.

削足适履

xuē zú shì lǚ

Cutting One's Feet to Fit One's Shoes

汉朝有一本叫《淮南子》的书，里面叙述了一个大傻瓜的故事：傻瓜去鞋店买鞋，店主拿给他一双鞋，鞋小了，他不是让店主去换，而是打算把自己的脚削去一块，以适合鞋的大小。傻瓜去帽店买帽，帽子小了，他又打算把自己的头皮削去一点，以适合帽子的大小。

"削足适履"比喻办事情不顾实际情况，生搬硬套，或比喻不合理的迁就。

The Han Dynasty (206 BC-220 AD) book titled *Huai Nan Zi* contains a story about a foolish man who went out to buy shoes. The shopkeeper handed him a pair that was small. The foolish man, instead of asking for another pair, tried to cut his feet to fit the shoes. When the foolish man went to buy a cap, the first cap he tried was too small, so he tried to cut off his scalp so that the cap would fit.

This idiom satirizes those who handle things without considering the actual situation, but rigidly apply unsuitable rules.

履：鞋。

Shoes.

揠苗助长

yà miáo zhù zhǎng

Pulling Up Seedlings to Help Them Grow

春秋时代，宋国有个急性子的种田人，庄稼长出禾苗以后，他每天都去观看，总嫌禾苗长得太慢。一天，他跑到田里去，把禾苗一棵棵往上拔。然后很疲倦地回到家，对家里人说："今天我帮助禾苗长高了！"家里人一听，赶忙跑到田里去看，禾苗全都枯萎(wěi)了。

"揠苗助长"这个成语，现在多写成"拔苗助长"，比喻违背事物发展的客观规律，急于求成，反而把事情弄糟。

In the Spring and Autumn Period, there was a farmer who was impatient by nature. He thought his rice shoots were growing too slowly, so he decided to help them by pulling them. One day at dusk, he went back home dog-tired and said to his family: "I helped the rice shoots grow today." Hearing this, his son hurried to the field, only to find that all the plants had withered.

This idiom is now often written 拔苗助长. It refers to spoiling things because of being over-anxious for results and ignoring the law of nature.

揠：拔。

To pull.

掩耳盗铃

yǎn ěr dào líng

Plugging One's Ears While Stealing a Bell

春秋时代，晋国有一个人看中了别人的一口铜钟，想把它偷回自己家里。钟又大又重，抱不动也背不动。他脑子一转，想出一个办法：把钟砸碎，再一块一块地拿回家。于是他拿起锤子就砸。刚一砸，钟就发出"当、当、当"的响声。他怕别人听见，急忙把自己的耳朵堵了起来。这个人以为自己听不见别人也就听不见了。

"掩耳盗钟"后来变成"掩耳盗铃"，用来讽刺自作聪明、自己欺骗自己。

In the Spring and Autumn Period, a man in the State of Jin took a fancy to a bronze bell and wanted to steal it. The bell was too large and heavy to be moved away, so he decided to smash it to pieces. But when his hammer struck the bell, it gave out a deep booming sound. Fearing that he might be heard, he covered his ears, and carried on with the work.

This idiom comes from the above story. It is used to satirize those who think they are smart but only deceive themselves.

偃旗息鼓

yǎn qí xī gǔ

To Lower the Banners and Silence the Drums

三国时代,一次曹操与刘备交战。刘备命令大将赵云、黄忠去抢夺曹操的粮食。曹操带领大军追赶赵云。赵云边打边退,一直退到营寨前,叫士兵打开营门,放倒军旗,停止擂鼓,在营外设好埋伏。曹军追到,看到这种情景,怀疑有埋伏,就撤退了。

“偃旗息鼓”这个成语现在用来比喻停止攻击或者事情中止。

In the Three Kingdoms Period, during a battle between Cao Cao and Liu Bei, the latter ordered his generals Zhao Yun and Huang Zhong to capture Cao Cao's supplies. Cao Cao led a large force against Zhao Yun, who retreated as far as the gates of his camp. There, he ordered that the banners be lowered and the war drums silenced, and that the camp gates be left wide open. Zhao Yun then stationed his troops in ambush nearly. When Cao Cao arrived and saw the situation, he immediately suspected a trap and withdrew his forces.

This idiom is nowadays used to indicate metaphorically halting an attack or ceasing all activities.

偃:放倒。

To lay down.

息:停止。

To stop.

叶公好龙

Yègōng hào lóng

Lord Ye Loves Dragons

传说古代有个叶公,非常喜欢龙。他家里的墙上、柱子上、门窗上到处都画满了龙,连日常生活用的东西上也画着龙。天上的真龙知道了。非常感动,就下降到他住的地方,将头伸进窗户,尾巴拖在厅堂。叶公一见真龙,吓得脸都变了颜色,拔腿就跑。

"叶公好龙"这个成语比喻表面上爱好某种事物,但实际上并不真正爱好。或者假装爱好,实际惧怕。

In ancient times there was a man called Ye Gong who was very fond of dragons. In his home everything, including the walls, windows, doors and even articles of daily use, were decorated with dragon designs. A real dragon was quite impressed when it heard about this, so it went to visit Ye Gong. However, when it stuck its head through the window Ye Gong was frightened and ran away.

This idiom satirizes those who profess to like or support something, but are averse to it in actual practice.

夜郎自大

Yèláng zì dà

The Conceited King of Yelang

在汉朝时，西南边境上有一个小国，叫夜郎国。这个国家虽然很小，但是国王却很骄傲，自以为他的国家很大，很了不起。有一次，汉朝的使者访问夜郎国，国王问使者："汉朝与我们夜郎国比较，哪一个大呢?"

后来人们就把本来没有什么能耐，却自以为很了不起而瞧不起别人，说成"夜郎自大"。

In the Han Dynasty, there was a tiny country called Yelang on the southwestern border. Small though it was, its ruler was quite proud of his country, thinking it big and powerful. Once a Han envoy visited Yelang. The ruler asked him: "Which is bigger, Han or Yelang?"

Later this idiom came to be used to refer to those who are capable of nothing yet are conceited.

一鼓作气

yī gǔ zuò qì

Rousing the Spirits with the First Drum Roll

春秋时代,齐国派兵攻打鲁国。鲁国的国王鲁庄公带着谋士曹刿(guì)指挥作战。齐军第一次击鼓以后,鲁军准备发起进攻。曹刿说:“不行。”齐军三次击鼓以后,曹刿才说:“现在可以进攻了。”结果齐军大败。战斗结束后,鲁庄公问曹刿胜利的原因。曹刿说:“打仗要靠勇气。第一次击鼓,士气十分旺盛;第二次击鼓,士气有些衰落;第三次击鼓,士气就耗尽了。敌人士气耗尽,我们发起进攻,所以取得了胜利。”

后来,“一鼓作气”形容鼓起劲头,一下子把事情干完。

During the Spring and Autumn Period, an army from the State of Qi confronted one from the State of Lu. After the first roll of drums from the Qi side to summon Lu to battle, the Lu ruler wanted to attack. But his counsellor Cao Gui said, “We should wait until the third drum roll, sire.” After the Qi side had beaten the drums three times, the Lu army attacked and defeated the Qi army. After the battle, the king asked Cao Gui the reason for his odd advice. Cao Gui answered, “Fighting needs spirit. Their spirit was aroused by the first roll of the drums, but was depleted by the second. And it was completely exhausted by the third. We started to attack when their spirit was exhausted. That's why we won.”

This idiom later meant to get something done with one sustained effort.

一箭双雕

yī jiàn shuāng diāo

Killing Two Birds with One Stone

南北朝时代，有个名叫长（Zhǎng）孙晟(shèng)的人，聪明敏捷，特别善于射箭。一天他同朋友一起去打猎，忽然看见两只雕在空中争夺一块肉。他的朋友立即给了长孙晟两只箭，说："你能把两只雕都射下来吗?"长孙晟不慌不忙拉开弓，只射了一箭，就把两只雕同时射下来了。朋友直夸他好箭法。

"一箭双雕"比喻用一种办法同时得到两种收获或效果。

In the period of the Northern and Southern Dynasties (420-589) there was an expert archer named Zhangsun Cheng. One day he went hunting together with a friend. Suddenly they saw two vultures fighting for a piece of meat high in the air. His friend handed him two arrows, and said, "Can you shoot down both vultures?" Zhangsun Cheng effortlessly killed both vultures with only one arrow.

This idiom indicates achieving two things with one stroke.

一鸣惊人

yī míng jīng rén

Amazing the World with a Single Feat

战国时代，齐威王即位后做了三年国君，只顾享乐，不理政事。有个善于说笑话的人叫淳(Chún)于髡(kūn)，一天对齐威王说："城里有一只大鸟，三年不飞也不叫，你知道这是什么道理？"齐威王说："这鸟不飞则罢，一飞就冲天；不鸣则罢，一鸣就惊人。"在淳于髡的激发下，齐威王开始治理国家，取得很大成绩，齐国的声威一直保持了几十年。

"一鸣惊人"用来表示平时默默无闻，一旦行动起来，却做出惊人的成绩。

In the Warring States Period, Duke Wei of Qi neglected state affairs, for the first three years of his reign, giving himself over to dissipation. One of his ministers, Chun Yukun who had a good sense of humour, said to him: "There is a big bird which has neither taken wing nor sung for three years." The duke answered, "Once that bird starts to fly and sing, it will astonish the world." The duke thereupon devoted himself to his duties and built his state up into a powerful one.

This idiom is used to indicate that a person may rise from obscurity and achieve greatness.

一丘之貉

yī qiū zhī hé

Jackals of the Same Lair

汉朝时,有个叫杨恽(yùn)的人,在朝廷做官,廉洁无私,又很有才能。有一次,他听说一个小国王被杀死,就发表议论说:“君王不采纳贤臣的计策,就会得到这种下场。秦朝皇帝宠信奸臣,所以亡国;如果重用贤臣,他的国家就不会亡了。”他最后总结说,古今的帝王都不过是一个山丘上的貉而已。

“一丘之貉”这个成语比喻某些人彼此相同,或者都是坏人。

In the Han Dynasty, there was an official called Yang Yun who was both capable and honest. Commenting on the assassination of a king of a small state, he said, “If a king refuses to follow the advice of a wise minister, he will suffer an untimely death. The emperor of the Qin Dynasty trusted treacherous ministers, and therefore lost his state.” He compared kings and emperors to racoons living on the same mountain.

This idiom refers derogatorily to people who are of the same kind.

貉:一种哺乳动物。

Racoon dog.

愚公移山

Yúgōng yí shān

The Foolish Old Man Who Removed the Mountains

古代有个愚公,家门前有两座大山挡住去路,出门很不方便。愚公决心率领他的子孙们挖掉这两座大山。有个智叟劝阻他说:“你太傻了。像你这么大年纪,连小山都平不了,还想搬走两座大山?”愚公笑笑说:“我死了有儿子,儿子死了有孙子,子子孙孙无穷无尽,而山不会增高了,还愁把它挖不平?”愚公的精神感动了天帝,于是天帝派了两个神仙把两座山搬走了。

“愚公移山”比喻做事有顽强的毅力,不怕困难,坚持到底。

In ancient times, there was an old man in front of whose house were two high mountains, making it very inconvenient for him to come and go. He gathered his family and started to level the mountains. His neighbour scoffed, "You are foolish. You are too old and weak to level a small hill, let alone two big mountains." But the old man said, "I have sons, and my sons have sons. I will have endless progeny, but the mountains won't grow any higher." The spirit of the "Foolish Old Man" moved Heaven, and it sent two immortals to move the mountains away.

This idiom describes an indomitable will.

鱼目混珠

yú mù hùn zhū

Passing Off Fish Eyes as Pearls

汉朝时候有个叫魏伯阳的人，写了一本讲述道家炼丹的书。在这本书里有两句很有意思的话："鱼目怎么能混同于珍珠，蓬蒿(pénghāo)绝不能冒充茶树。"鱼的眼睛和珍珠看起来有点相像，但是价值就大不相同了。

"鱼目混珠"这个成语，比喻用假的东西冒充真的东西。

In the Han Dynasty, there was a Taoist called Wei Boyang who wrote a book on the making of pills of immortality. In this book there is the following line: "Fish eyes can't be passed off as pearls, and bitter flea-bane can't pretend to be tea." Fish eyes look like pearls, but are valueless.

This idiom is used to mean passing off the sham as the genuine.

余音绕梁

yú yīn rào liáng

The Tune Lingers in the House

战国时候,韩国有个女子名叫韩娥。她的嗓音很好,唱起歌来,美妙动听。有一次她出门经过齐国,粮食吃完了,只好靠卖唱来维持生活。不久之后,韩娥离开了齐国,可是她的歌声却还回荡在人们的屋梁附近,一直过了三天都没有消失。齐国的人们都以为韩娥还没有走呢。

"余音绕梁"这个成语用来形容歌声优美,使人很久不能忘怀。

In the Warring States Period, there was a girl in the State of Han called Han E who sang beautifully. Once when she was passing through the State of Qi she had to sing to earn money to buy food. When she left Qi the echoes of her songs clung to the beams of the houses there for three days before people realized that she had left.

This idiom is used to describe unforgettably beautiful singing.

与虎谋皮

yǔ hǔ móu pí

Borrowing the Skin from a Tiger

传说古代有个人非常爱好皮衣和珍异的美味。他想做一件价值千金的皮衣,就去跟狐狸商量要它的皮。他想吃鲜美的羊肉,就去跟羊商量要它的肉。狐狸和羊听见他说这样的话,都逃到远远的地方去了。

这个故事原来叫"与狐谋皮",后来转化成"与虎谋皮",比喻跟恶人商量要他牺牲自己的利益,那是绝对办不到的。

In ancient times there was a man who was very fond of fur clothes and fine food. He asked a fox to give him its pelt, but the fox ran away. He then asked a sheep for its meat, but the sheep too ran away.

与狐谋皮, later known as 与虎谋皮, means that it is impossible to discuss with the vicious about getting profits from them.

鹬蚌相争

yù bàng xiāng zhēng

A Snipe and a Clam Locked in Combat

一只河蚌张开了壳,在河滩上晒太阳。忽然一只鹬猛地把尖尖的嘴伸过来啄蚌的肉。蚌立刻合拢它的壳,紧紧地夹住了鹬的嘴。鹬说:“今天不下雨,明天不下雨,你就会被太阳晒死!”蚌说:“你的嘴今天不出来,明天不出来,你就会饿死!”双方互不相让,正巧走过来一个渔夫,就把它们一同捉走了。

“鹬蚌相争”比喻双方相持不下,两败俱伤,让第三者得到了好处。

One day a clam opened its shell to sunbathe on a beach. Suddenly a snipe stuck its beak in the clam. The latter closed its shell immediately, and trapped the snipe's beak. The clam refused to open its shell, and the snipe refused to remove its beak. Neither of them would concede defeat. Finally, a fisherman came along and caught both of them.

This idiom means that if two sides contend, it is a third party that benefits.

鹬:吃鱼类、贝类的鸟。

Snipe.

蚌:带壳的软体动物。

Clam.

朝三暮四

zhāo sān mù sì

Three in the Morning and Four in the Evening

春秋时代，宋国有一个人，养了一大群猴子。这些猴子能够听懂主人说的话。过了一段时间，主人家里穷了，想限制一下猴子每天吃的粮食。于是对猴子说："每天给你们吃的橡（xiàng）子，早上三个，晚上四个，够了吗？"猴子们听了，都怒气冲冲地站了起来。主人又说："早上四个，晚上三个，够了吗？"猴子们听了，都趴（pā）在地上表示满意。

"朝三暮四"原来表示欺骗和愚弄的手段，以后改用来比喻说话、做事反复无常。

In the Spring and Autumn Period, a man in the State of Song raised monkeys. The monkeys could understand what he said. As the man became poor, he wanted to reduce the monkeys' food. He first suggested that he give them four acorns in the morning and three acorns in the evening. Thereupon, the monkeys protested angrily. Then their owner said, "How about three in the morning and four in the evening?" The monkeys were satisfied with that.

This idiom originally meant to befool others with tricks. Later it is used to mean to keep changing one's mind.

趾高气扬

zhǐ gāo qì yáng

Stepping High and Haughtily

春秋时代,楚国出兵攻打罗国。一个名叫斗伯比的官员去送行,看到带兵的主帅的样子,回来后私下对人说:“这次出征,主帅走路时脚抬得高高的,一副神气十足、傲慢轻敌的样子。这样恐怕是要打败仗的!”果然不出所料,这次战斗,楚国大败,连主帅也自杀了。

“趾高气扬”这个成语用来形容骄傲自满、得意忘形。

In the Spring and Autumn Period, the State of Chu sent troops to attack the State of Luo. An official called Dou Bobi went to see the troops off. When he came back, he said to someone secretly: “The general walked in an arrogant way, stepping high. I'm afraid he will be defeated.” Sure enough, the Chu troops were badly defeated, and the general committed suicide.

This idiom is used to describe being arrogant and putting on airs.

趾:脚。

Foot.

指鹿为马

zhǐ lù wéi mǎ

Calling a Stag a Horse

秦朝丞相赵高想篡（cuàn）夺帝位，怕群臣们不服气，就想了一个办法来试一试大家。他牵来一只鹿献给皇帝说："这是一匹马。"皇帝笑着说："丞相你弄错了吧？这是一只鹿。"赵高就问旁边的大臣们。他们有的不做声，有的跟着赵高说是马，也有说是鹿的。凡是说鹿的人，后来都被赵高杀了。从此以后，群臣都害怕赵高。

"指鹿为马"用来比喻故意颠倒黑白，混淆（xiáo）是非。

In the Qin Dynasty, the prime minister, Zhao Gao, plotted to usurp the throne. Fearing that the other ministers would oppose this, he thought of a way of testing them. He presented a deer to the emperor, and said, "This is a horse." The emperor laughed, and said, "You must be joking; this is a deer." Then Zhao Gao asked the ministers present. Some kept silent, some said that it was a deer, and others agreed that it was a horse.

Later Zhao Gao had all the ministers who had not said that it was a horse killed.

This metaphor describes distorting facts by calling white black.

纸上谈兵

zhǐ shàng tán bīng

Discussing Strategems on Paper

战国时，赵国名将赵奢（shē）的儿子赵括，喜欢看兵书，谈兵法。他把兵书背得滚瓜烂熟，谈起打仗来头头是道，似乎他的父亲也比不过他。一次秦国攻打赵国，赵王派赵括率领四十万大军去抵抗。由于他只知道死抠书本而不会在实际中灵活运用，最后指挥失策，以致全军覆灭，他自己也中箭身亡。

后来人们根据这一历史故事，把死抠书本，没有实践经验，只会夸夸其谈称为“纸上谈兵”。

In the Warring States Period, the State of Zhao had a famous general called Zhao She, whose son, Zhao Kuo, was very fond of reading books on military science and discussing strategy. He could recite military texts by heart, and when discussing warfare he spoke so clearly and logically that it seemed that even his father was not his match. When the State of Qin attacked the State of Zhao, the ruler of Zhao ordered Zhao Kuo to lead 400, 000 men to resist the attack. But since Zhao Kuo had no practical experience of battle, he was defeated and lost his life.

Later people used this idiom to describe those who are good only at theorizing, and lack practical experience.

兵：兵法，兵书。

(Here) art of war; book on art of war.

自相矛盾

zì xiāng máodùn

Contradicting Oneself

古代有个卖矛和盾的人。他一手举起他的矛夸耀说:“我的矛锋利无比,无论多么坚硬的东西都能刺穿。”过了一会,他又举起另一只手里的盾说:“我的盾坚硬无比,无论多么锋利的东西也刺不破。”观众中有一个人问他:“用你的矛刺你的盾,结果会怎样呢?”这个人被问得哑口无言了。

“自相矛盾”用来比喻说话或做事不一致,互相抵触。

In ancient times, there was a man who sold spears and shields. He used to boast, “My spears are the sharpest things in the world. They can penetrate anything.” A moment later he would boast, “My shields are the toughest things in the world. Nothing can penetrate them.” One day, a passer-by asked him: “What would happen if you threw one of your spears at one of your shields?”

This idiom, “contradicting oneself”, and the noun 矛盾, contradiction, all came from the above story.

图书在版编目(CIP)数据

成语100:汉英对照/尹斌庸编著.—北京:华语教学出版社,1999.8

(博古通今学汉语丛书)

ISBN 7-80052-708-5

Ⅰ.成… Ⅱ.尹… Ⅲ.对外汉语教学—成语—对照读物—英、汉

Ⅳ.H195.5

中国版本图书馆 CIP 数据核字(1999)第 08151 号

博古通今学汉语丛书

成语 100

*

华语教学出版社出版

(中国北京百万庄路 24 号)

邮政编码 100037

电话:86-010-68326333/68996153

传真:86-010-68994599

电子信箱:sinolingua@ihw.com.cn

北京外文印刷厂印刷

中国国际图书贸易总公司海外发行

(中国北京车公庄西路 35 号)

北京邮政信箱第 399 号　邮政编码 100044

新华书店国内发行

1999 年(34 开)第一版

2000 年第二次印刷

2001 年第三次印刷

(汉英)

ISBN 7-80052-708-5/H·778(外)

01600(平)

9-CE-3330P